P9-DWT-670

Contents

Preface to Part Two

The exercises in these two volumes of *Kum Nye Relaxation* have developed during ten years of classes and programs at the Nyingma Institute in Berkeley. Kum Nye is a holistic system which vitalizes body, mind, and senses by means of breathing exercises, self-massage, and movement. The massages and exercises included in these two volumes show us how to develop the special nurturing qualities of relaxation, and to bring this relaxation into our daily lives. Kum Nye is not an advanced or esoteric practice, but a simple method of opening our senses to inner feelings of satisfaction and fulfillment. As these feelings expand, an understanding of the unity of all experience develops, and daily life takes on a vital, balanced quality.

The exercises in this second volume are most effective if they are practiced after an understanding of Kum Nye has already begun to be incorporated in the body. First, practice the breathing and massages of Part 1; then begin to practice some of these exercises. Do not feel that you must learn all of the exercises; doing a few of them well can be a most fruitful approach.

Kum Nye Relaxation can be used not only as a

Kum Nye Relaxation

Feelings of love and openness nourish and renew us,
radiating to the surrounding environment.

Kum Nye Relaxation

Part 2:
Movement Exercises

Tarthang Tulku

Dharma Publishing

 NYINGMA PSYCHOLOGY SERIES

Reflections of Mind
Gesture of Balance
Openness Mind
Kum Nye Relaxation, Parts 1 and 2
Skillful Means

Library of Congress Cataloging in Publication Data

Tarthang Tulku.
  Kum Nye relaxation.

  (Nyingma Psychology Series; 4)
  Includes index.
  1. Relaxation.   2. Mind and body.   3. Exercise.
4. Massage.   I. Title.
RA785.T37   613.7′9   78-10418
ISBN 0-913546-10-0 (v. 1)
ISBN 0-913546-25-9 pbk. (v. 1)
ISBN 0-913546-75-5 (v. 2)
ISBN 0-913546-74-7 pbk. (v. 2)

Copyright © 1978 Dharma Publishing
All rights reserved. No part of this book,
either text or art, may be reproduced in any form
without written permission. For information address:
Dharma Publishing, 2425 Hillside Ave.,
Berkeley, California 94704 USA

Editing, illustration, and design by Dharma Publishing
Typeset in Fototronic Medallion, printed, and bound by
Dharma Press, Emeryville, California

9 8 7 6 5 4 3 2 1

manual for teaching oneself to balance and integrate body and mind, but also as a teaching text in traditional learning environments, each volume corresponding to a semester course. These two volumes give a basic introduction to Kum Nye. Kum Nye also includes visualization, breathing, and therapeutic exercises which need more specific guidance than can be given in a book of this kind. Professionals who are interested in teaching Kum Nye or in using Kum Nye in their work should contact the Nyingma Institute in Berkeley for information on Kum Nye classes and training programs.

Readers who are interested in meditation will find this a useful book, for Kum Nye leads naturally to meditation. But because Kum Nye is not specifically directed toward spiritual development, those who are interested in exploring meditative techniques will find more information in two of my other books, *Gesture of Balance* and *Openness Mind*.

I wish to thank all those who have waited so patiently for this book. I want also to give my heartfelt thanks to my students and friends at Dharma Publishing and Dharma Press who put such tremendous and inspired effort into producing these volumes. All of the many processes involved—editing, illustrating, designing, typesetting, and printing, etc.—required a level of cooperation which I deeply appreciate. Without such help, this book would not have been possible.

Tarthang Tulku
September, 1978

Exercises

Stimulating Energies: Stage Three

Kum Nye Relaxation

Balancing and Integrating Body, Mind, and Senses

Balance is a natural condition of flowing feeling and energy which pervades the entire body and mind.

We commonly think of balance as our bodily equilibrium or stability. This understanding of balance is limited, however, and can be expanded by certain exercises and movements which show us how to bring our breath, senses, and awareness into balance with our bodies and minds. We can make our whole system balanced, for balance is a natural condition of flowing feeling and energy which pervades the entire body and mind. This balance is the objective of Kum Nye.

The foundation of balance and the integration of body and mind is relaxation. Often we think of relaxation as a state of dreaminess, lacking in awareness and vitality; or a process of escaping from life; or a filling or a marking out of time. But true relaxation is actually balance. When we are relaxed, we can open to new sensory fields and dimensions, expanding sensations and feelings which bring body and mind together. We learn to generate and accumulate energy, using it so that both body and mind work together in a flowing, open way. Thoughts and sensations flow smoothly because the mind is vibrant and clear, and the body vital and energetic. When we truly relax, it is no longer the 'self' that is experiencing—we become the experience itself. We no longer 'own' our senses, bodies, and minds, for they all totally participate in the experience.

Often, however, our minds and bodies do not communicate well with each other, and we are unable to nourish either one properly. We then cannot sustain our vitality, our concentration, or awareness, so we function ineffectively and become prone to mental and physical imbalances. Most psychological problems and most illnesses—including the diseases of stress—are related to these subtle energy imbalances in our bodies, minds, and senses. Our sensations become confused, and our energy scattered and unsteady. Lacking vital awareness, our bodies and senses are like unused houses . . . mental, physical, and sensory awareness diminishes. Strong emotions aggravate the situation.

The integration and balancing of physical and mental energies frees us from these patterns. We become able to flow with experience, allowing it to nourish and satisfy us. Our perspective changes, and we learn to understand things in new ways—we see that neither the good nor the bad experiences last for long, and we become less subject to emotional extremes. We do not try to control or fix our experience, for we possess a knowledge based on opening to each situation in our lives as an opportunity for growth. We open to the vital and wholesome nature of all experience, and can then see the preciousness and grace of every aspect of life. Our inner peacefulness shows us the harmony of existence, and everything becomes relevant to our lives. We come to appreciate every person, situation, sensation, and feeling in our lives, even those we call 'negative'.

When our relationships to the world become more flowing and complete, our ability to communicate improves, and we are less dependent on others to protect our sense of well-being and happiness. We become willing to expand beyond the limited space and time of our usual sense of 'privacy', expanding also our senses, feelings, thoughts, and awareness. Eventually we discover there is an infinite sort of knowledge available which itself can be extended, and which gives us a way of understanding the beauty, richness, and value of our inner resources.

The exercises in this chapter are divided into three stages. There is a progression within each stage, and from stage to stage. If you wish, do the exercises in the order they are presented; however, do not feel that you must do them in this progression. Some exercises will suit you better than others, and it is perfectly all right to do the exercises within a stage in a different sequence, or to practice some of the exercises in Stage Two or even Stage Three before doing all of the exercises in Stage One. Feel free to experiment with different combinations of exercises. Let your body lead you to those exercises that stimulate the most vital feeling for you, and vary the sequence and combination of exercises enough so that your practice is interesting and balanced.

If you can, allow forty-five minutes a day for practice; if you cannot spare that much time, twenty to thirty minutes will also bring results. Begin by practicing two or three exercises each day, doing each exercise three times. Choose three or four exercises that you like, and stay with them until you feel confident you have touched your feelings deeply. This may take two or three weeks. Then over the next six or eight weeks, gradually increase your vocabulary of exercises to approximately ten. Practice some of the standing exercises as well as the sitting ones; at times you may also want to do some massage or a breathing exercise along with the movement exercises.

Whatever sequence or combination of exercises you choose, do not be in a rush. Coverage and speed are not important. Remember that these exercises are different from ordinary physical exercises; they are not designed simply to improve the physical functioning of the body. They will do this, but when practiced properly, they will also awaken the senses, stimulating certain feeling-tones which, when cultivated and extended, improve the functioning of the total organism—body, mind, and senses.

Each exercise is a symbol which leads to special energies or feeling tones. As you practice an exercise, develop the qualities of your feelings as fully as you can. Be sensitive to your own experience. If your feelings or sensations do not match the feelings or sensations mentioned in the exercise descriptions, do not be concerned; these descriptions are only indications of what you might feel. Bring your breath and your awareness to each feeling, and allow its special tones to permeate your body and mind.

As your feelings expand, you will become familiar with different stages of relaxation. When you begin an exercise, you may find that you are watching yourself do the exercise; there is a division between you and your sensations. As you continue to relax and are able to explore a movement with light concentration, simultaneously breathing at an even level and expanding the sensations stimulated by the exercise, experience becomes richer and more substantial in quality; a feeling of 'the exercise doing itself' begins.

Each repetition of the exercise then becomes an opportunity to explore more fully the feelings activated by the movement, a chance to bring body, mind, and senses together. Mental and physical energies contact each other and become integrated. Later, there may be no sense of 'self' at all, only ever-expanding awareness.

You may find that some of the exercises have an immediate effect; others may affect you gradually. Certain exercises may not seem to affect you at all, even after several practice sessions. If an exercise does not seem to generate much feeling or energy, you may be holding tension somewhere which blocks the flow of sensation. Perhaps you are holding a particular position too rigidly. Try moving a little within the position; a tension may relax and release a different quality of energy. If the exercise continues to have little effect, let it go for a while. Later you may return to an exercise you earlier set aside and find it effective.

Continue to explore your feelings in a sensitive way during the sitting period of each exercise. The sitting posture described in Part 1, i.e. the seven gestures, will encourage an even flow of feeling throughout your body. If you wish, sit before practicing as well. Sit and move within your feelings; develop a meditative awareness. When you finish practicing, let your next activity also be a form of Kum Nye. Expand your feelings while eating, walking, or seeing. Let relaxation inform every experience, so your whole life becomes part of an expanding, widening meditation.

Stage One

As you begin these exercises, remember to wear loose, comfortable clothing or a leotard; tight clothes (especially clothes tight around the waist) will restrict your movement and distract you from the feelings generated by the exercise. Remove shoes, watches, jewelry, glasses, or contact lenses. If you eat beforehand, eat lightly, and wait for at least an hour after eating to begin practice.

Some of these exercises are done sitting, some are done standing. For the sitting exercises, you will need a mat or cushion so that your pelvis is higher than your legs. You may want to experiment with different ways of sitting and crossing your legs until you find the position that permits the most ease of movement. If sitting cross-legged is too uncomfortable for you, then sit in a straight chair with your feet flat on the floor.

Most of the exercises in this stage release tension in the upper body—the shoulders, chest, back, arms, neck, and head. As tension in these areas lessens, it is possible to feel more in the heart. These exercises develop valuable healing energies, so be sure to go deeply into some of them. You will find them most effective if you have already developed the massage and some of the exercises in Part 1 of this book.

Practice as regularly as you can. If you miss a day or so, do not be concerned; you will not lose ground. Encourage yourself and continue to practice. When you are very busy, doing an exercise even for five or ten minutes on a break from work will have a beneficial effect.

At times you may find that you are unable to touch your feelings during an exercise. This may indicate that your body and mind are too excited or tense to communicate well with each other. Your mind may be so full of thoughts and images that you are unable to sense your feelings clearly. You may be too upset to breathe in the even and gentle way that awakens nurturing feelings. This unsteady state of mind will most likely cause your physical balance to be unsteady as well.

When you are feeling 'off balance', sit quietly for a while before exercising, and concentrate lightly on your breathing. Let your breath become light and soft. When you begin to feel more relaxed and calm, slowly begin an exercise. As relaxation deepens, a flowing, moving quality like waves may arise. The feeling may be smooth and flowing, almost magically sweet. With regular practice this feeling can be expanded and relaxation will deepen until you find that this flowing rhythm has passed into all of your daily activities.

Exercise 35   Loosening Up the Mind

If you are pregnant or have had any kind of neck injury, it is best not to do this exercise.

Sit cross-legged on a mat or cushion with your back straight. Slowly lift your arms away from your sides until they are stretched out at shoulder height, palms down. Close your eyes. Breathing softly through both nose and mouth, very slowly begin to rotate your head in a clockwise direction. As you complete the first rotation, also begin to rotate your right arm up, back, down, and forward. Coordinate the two circles, making them large and full.

This movement may seem awkward or even difficult at first, for we are not accustomed to moving our heads and arms in this way. Your mind may be set in a familiar pattern of movement which you feel unwilling to change. Use the movement to 'exercise' the feeling of unwillingness until it changes into a natural flow of feeling and energy. Relax your belly, and let your breath become very even. Bring this even breath into the movement, so the rotations become smooth and spacious.

Make three slow coordinated rotations of the head and right arm; then find a place in the movement where you can comfortably change the direction of the circles of both head and arm, and make three slow rotations in the other direction. Be sure to keep your left arm outstretched at shoulder height throughout; this will make the movement easier.

Go deeply into the sensations generated by the movement, unifying body, breath, and mind. You may feel a delicious warmth in your arms and at the back of your neck. Let the warmth flow down your spine and spread throughout your body.

When you finish the rotations, slowly lower your hands to your knees. Rest for a few minutes, continuing to expand the feelings within and around your body. If you want to, also lower your hands to your knees and rest briefly before changing the direction of the rotations.

Now repeat the above sequence of rotations with the head and the left arm. Rest afterward for a few minutes, breathing gently and evenly.

To complete the exercise, again do the whole series of rotations, but this time with the head and arm moving in opposite directions from each other: when the head moves clockwise, the arm will move forward, down, back, and up. Begin with your head and right arm, rest for a few minutes with your hands on your knees, and repeat the movement with the head and left arm. Remember to keep your breathing soft and even, uniting it with your sensations. At the end, sit quietly for five to ten minutes, amplifying and extending your sensations and feelings.

Exercise 36   Awakening the Senses

If you are pregnant or have had any kind of neck injury, it is best not to do this exercise.

Sit cross-legged on a mat or cushion with your back straight. Lift your arms away from your sides a few inches, with the palms facing behind you. Be sure your pelvis is high enough to allow your arms to move without your hands touching the floor.

Gently close your eyes, and very slowly begin to rotate your right shoulder up, back, down, and forward. Your right hand will also move in a circle. As you complete the first rotation, also begin to rotate your head in a clockwise direction. Coordinate the two movements, making the circles as full as you can. As you move, breathe gently through both nose and mouth, and concentrate lightly on the back of your neck. Make three coordinated rotations, then gently change the direction of the rotations of both shoulder and head, and continue three more times. After finishing, put your hands on your knees and rest briefly, allowing the feelings awakened by the slow rotations to flow down your spine, and be distributed throughout your body.

Now in the same way as before, lift your arms away from your sides a few inches with the palms facing behind you, and very slowly rotate your left shoulder—up, back, down, and forward—coordinating the movement with a clockwise rotation of your head. Make three rotations in this way; then gently change the direction of the rotations and repeat three times. After completing these movements, bring your hands to your knees and rest for a few minutes, continuing to expand your sensations.

To complete the exercise, again do the whole series of rotations, but this time with the shoulder and head moving in opposite directions from each other: when the shoulder moves up, back, down, and forward, the head will move counterclockwise. Begin with the right shoulder and head, rest for a few minutes with your hands on your knees, and repeat the movement with the left shoulder and head. Develop the shape of the movement, with special attention to the high and low points (when the head is at its highest point in the movement, the shoulder is lowest and vice versa), and the points when the head and shoulder are nearest and farthest from each other. Allow the feelings generated by the movement to permeate the shape until you experience a 'feeling-shape'.

Now sit in the sitting posture for five to ten minutes, enlarging and deepening the sensations within and around your body.

This exercise releases tension in the back of the neck, the shoulders, the upper back, and sometimes the lower back.

Exercise 37   Balancing the Senses

If you are pregnant or have had any kind of neck injury, it is best not to do this exercise.

Sit cross-legged on a mat or cushion with your back straight and your hands on your knees. Lift your arms in front of you to chest height with your elbows loosely bent and your hands relaxed, the palms down, and the fingers pointing forward. Picture two large clockfaces side by side facing you. Imagine that your left hand is at three on the left clockface, and your right hand is at nine on the right clockface. Your hands will be a few inches apart.

Now at the same time, very slowly, draw two large clockwise circles with your hands and arms, beginning at three and moving toward six with the left hand, and beginning at nine and moving toward twelve with the right hand. Make the circles as large as possible without overlapping them.

When you have this movement going in a smooth rhythm, add to it a very slow clockwise rotation of your head, with your eyes closed. Coordinate and balance the three simultaneous movements, keeping your belly relaxed, and your breathing very soft and smooth, through both nose and mouth. Continue for two minutes, then slowly diminish the movement until you no longer move at all. Lower your hands to your knees and sit for two minutes, expanding the sensations stimulated by these circling movements.

Now repeat the exercise, this time making counterclockwise circles with both the arms and the head (move the left hand from three toward twelve on the left clockface, and the right hand from nine toward six on the right clockface). Continue for two minutes, then sit quietly for five minutes, continuing to extend the sensations within and around your body. When you can balance your body and mind in coordinating three different movements at the same time, the senses also become balanced and sensations arise within balance.

Exercise 38 Enjoying Sensation

Stand well balanced with your feet a few inches apart, your back straight, and your arms relaxed at your sides. Breathing gently and evenly through both nose and mouth, with your belly relaxed, loosely and vigorously shake your shoulders in any way you wish. Relax the back of your neck, and concentrate lightly there, letting your head hang. Your torso and lower body remain still. Continue for three minutes, shaking out tightness. Then sit in the sitting posture for five minutes, expanding the sensations generated by this movement, distributing them throughout your body.

You may feel a deep, warm sensation in the back of your neck flowing down your spine, and perhaps spreading to your chest and arms. The flow of feeling through the neck to the head may be more free.

Exercise 39   Swimming in Space

Stand well balanced with your feet a comfortable
distance apart, your back straight, and your arms
stretched out in front of you at shoulder height, palms
down. Breathing easily through both nose and mouth,
with your belly relaxed, simultaneously move one
arm up and the other arm down, keeping the arms
and hands straight and relaxed.

Move very slowly. At first do not move the arms very far—then gradually extend the movement until finally each arm moves up and down as far as it can go. At the furthest points of the movement, relax the back of the neck and head. Pay attention to the particular sense of space awakened by this exercise; you may feel a quality like swimming.

Continue the full movement of the arms for three to five minutes, then slowly decrease the range of the movement until your arms are still, and extended in front of you at shoulder height. Slowly lower them to your sides, and stand quietly for a few minutes, expanding your sensations and feelings.

Now slowly lift your arms in front of you until they are overhead with the palms facing forward. Keep your arms parallel to each other and straight. Moving your arms, head, and torso together, bend down from the waist until your fingers almost touch the floor; then swing up slowly until your back is straight and your arms are outstretched overhead.

Continue this slow swinging movement, down and up, three or nine times. Be sure to keep the arms straight throughout the movement. To complete the exercise, lower your arms to your sides from the overhead position, and sit in the sitting posture for five to ten minutes, expanding the sensations quickened by this movement.

The first part of this exercise releases tension in the back, the throat, the neck, and the back of the head. The second part distributes the feelings released in the first part of the exercise throughout the whole body.

Exercise 40   Awareness of the Senses

This exercise differs from the preceding exercise in
the position of the hands and arms. Stand well
balanced with your feet a comfortable distance
apart, your back straight, and your arms relaxed at
your sides. Turn your hands inward until the palms
face out to the sides, and stick out your thumbs so
they also point out to the side. With your hands in

this position, slowly lift your arms in front of you to shoulder height. Breathe easily through both nose and mouth, and keep your belly relaxed.

Now, keeping your arms straight but relaxed, very slowly begin to move one arm up and the other arm down. Move them just a short distance at first, concentrating on the feelings in and around them as they move slowly through space. Gradually, as your feelings expand, extend the range of movement in your arms until they are both moving up and down as far as they will go. Expand fully the special qualities of feeling stimulated by this movement, keeping your belly relaxed and your breathing soft, even, and slow.

Continue for three to five minutes, then slowly decrease the range of the movement until your arms are still, outstretched in front of you at shoulder height. Slowly lower your arms to your sides, relax your hands, and stand quietly for a few minutes, expanding the feelings generated by this movement.

Once again turn your hands inward until the palms face out to the sides, and stick out your thumbs so they also point out to the side. With your hands in this position, slowly lift your arms in front of you until they are overhead, keeping them parallel to each other and straight. Then bend forward slowly from the waist until your fingers almost touch the floor.

Let your head hang loosely between your arms. Relax your belly and breathe easily through both nose and mouth. Then slowly rise with your head between your outstretched arms until you stand upright with your arms overhead. Continue to bend and rise slowly three times, sensing deeply the particular spatial quality stimulated by this position of the hands and arms.

Slowly begin to move slightly faster, swinging up and down, letting your feelings merge with the rhythm of your body. As you move faster, make sure that your belly stays relaxed, and your movement and breathing are smooth and even. If you begin to lose touch with the feeling quality of the movement, slow down until the sensations become stronger; then slowly build up more speed. Swing up and down nine more times. You may feel a special tingling sensation in your arms.

Then, from the upright position, slowly lower your arms to your sides, relax your hands, and stand quietly for a minute. Then sit in the sitting posture for five to ten minutes, breathing gently and evenly. Allow your sensations to be distributed throughout your body and to expand beyond your body to the surrounding universe.

Exercise 41   Body Alertness

Stand facing forward with your feet a few inches apart, your back straight, and your arms relaxed at your sides. Inhale through both nose and mouth, and slowly raise your arms in front of you to shoulder height, palms down. Keep your head and chest very still. As you exhale, very slowly move both arms to the right as far as possible, keeping the rest of your body, especially your chest, relaxed and still. Lead the movement with your right arm; the right arm will be straight, and the left arm will bend slightly at the elbow.

Now while inhaling, let your arms come back very slowly to the front; and without stopping, continue the movement to the left while exhaling. Lead the movement to the left with your left arm; the left arm will be straight, and the right arm bent slightly at the elbow. Throughout the movement, your belly should be relaxed and your body straight and well balanced.

Do the complete movement, once to each side, three or nine times. Then sit in the sitting posture for five to ten minutes with the feelings awakened by the exercise.

Exercise 42   Balancing the Body

Do this exercise barefoot. Stand well balanced with
your hands on your hips, your feet a few inches apart,
your back straight, and your chest high. Breathe
gently through both nose and mouth. Slowly lift your
right heel so your right toes and your left foot carry
your weight. Now in a slow, continuous motion, with
both feet always in contact with the floor, lower your

right heel to the floor and simultaneously lift your left heel. Continue in a slow, smooth rhythm, lifting the heel of one foot while lowering the heel of the other to the floor. Your weight and balance will be primarily on the toes and balls of the feet.

Notice the point at which you are standing on the toes of both feet, as one heel moves up and the other moves down. Intensify the 'high' at this point by stretching up on the toes. Then intensify the 'low' as well: as your heel comes back to the floor, push the hip on that side of your body back and down as if sitting down in a low chair, bending both knees. Keep your back straight. Notice the change in feeling-tone as the vertical range of the movement increases.

Continue this movement until it is no longer jerky or unbalanced, and both the breath and the movement are slow and smooth. Then (but not before) do the movement a little faster, but not so fast that you lose touch with the feeling-tone. Finally, slow down the movement until it stops altogether. Then sit for five to ten minutes in the sitting posture, expanding the sensations stimulated in your body, mind, and senses.

This exercise balances the body and stimulates energy in the toe, knee, thigh, and hip joints.

Exercise 43   Sensing Body Energy

Stand well balanced with your feet a comfortable distance apart and your arms relaxed at your sides. Close your eyes, and take a few moments to relax and sense your inner experience. What is your emotional state? Are you feeling calm, restless, tired? Is your mind filled with thoughts?

Now very slowly open your eyes, and slowly begin to move spontaneously in any way that feels relaxing. Breathe gently through both nose and mouth, and relax your belly. Perhaps make swinging or rotating motions, or gently twist, rock, bend, or sway. Let the feeling of relaxation guide and balance your movement. Allow the relaxed feeling to spread everywhere in your body—to your jaw, neck, shoulders, upper back, arms, elbows, wrists, fingers, middle back, lower back, pelvis, thighs, knees, ankles, and toes. Be attentive to every joint, and do any movement that increases the feeling of relaxation. Continue for five minutes or more.

Now slowly develop a different quality of movement—a short, fast, light motion. This is not a heavy motion like kicking, but more like a rhythmical shaking. Perhaps begin the movement in your legs and hands, and then allow it to spread to more and more of your body, until finally your whole body participates in the movement. When you find a tense spot, let the shaking gently open it up. Continue for several minutes, and then sit in the sitting posture for five to ten minutes with the feelings stimulated by the movement.

Stage Two

These exercises continue to release tension in the upper body, balancing inner energies so that feeling can flow more freely, and body and mind can make contact with one another. Exercises 52 and 55 energize the lower body.

Some of these exercises involve holding a position for a period of time. You may wish to measure the time by counting your outbreaths. Before beginning the exercise, time your breathing for a few minutes, and calculate your average number of outbreaths per minute.

When you release tension after holding, do so very slowly. When the process of releasing tension is slow, awareness of energy increases, and it is easier to continue the feelings, and distribute them to your whole body. Quick release cuts off the feelings of stimulation and exhilaration.

Fully explore each exercise you select to practice until you become familiar with the range of feelings it stimulates, and its special qualities of balance. Do not go too fast or try to do too much. If you begin to feel overwhelmed by the possibilities opening up to you in these exercises, stay with that feeling and bring it into your practice. Let your self-imposed limitations open into deeper feeling and sensation; allow yourself to be larger and larger until you see that all limitations are arbitrary and self-imposed, and your experience can be as large as the universe itself.

Exercise 44   Touching the Senses

Sit cross-legged on a mat or cushion with your hands on your knees and your back straight. In a continuous, coordinated movement, alternately rotate your shoulders from front to back, as if back-pedalling a bicycle. Move them quickly and a little roughly. Let your shoulders be very loose as you do this, and your head still. Picture the spine and the spaces between the vertebrae being massaged by the action of your shoulder blades. Continue for one minute.

Now gradually change the quality of the movement so it becomes gentler, longer and slower, more soothing and massage-like in quality. Let this massage stimulate your senses, relieving tension and awakening sensation even between layers of skin and muscle tissue. Sensations may also be quickened in the heart center, awakening perhaps a feeling of yearning. Continue this massage for three to five minutes and then sit quietly for an equal amount of time, expanding the feeling-tone developed by this exercise.

☆ To explore this exercise further, try this variation. Rotate your left shoulder front to back twenty-one times, then repeat with your right shoulder. Sit for two minutes, experiencing the sensations stimulated by the movement.

Again rotate your left shoulder as before, twenty-one times, this time more slowly. Repeat with your right shoulder. Then sit with your feelings for two minutes.

Repeat the movement, first with the left, then with the right shoulder, this time even more slowly. Then sit for five minutes with the feelings and sensations that have emerged from the movement.

These exercises can also be done standing.

Exercise 45   Balancing Inner Energy

It is best not to do this exercise if you are pregnant. If you have had a neck or back injury, or have had an operation within three or four months, do it mindfully.

In this exercise you will make a circle in front of your body with your chin. Sit cross-legged on a mat or cushion with your hands relaxed on your knees, and breathe evenly and gently through both nose and mouth. Slowly jut and stretch your chin directly forward as far as possible. Do not be afraid to stretch strenuously (unless you have had a neck or back injury; then do this very sensitively). Be sure that the chest and neck remain straight and only the jaw and chin move forward; the movement then has great strength and energy and leads to a certain quality of relaxation.

Maintaining the strenuous stretch, and breathing very, very softly through both nose and mouth, slowly move your chin down toward your chest. When your chin nears your chest, slowly draw it in as close as possible to your neck. The muscles of the back of your neck will become very tense and strong, and may shimmy a little. Maintain this quality of strength in the neck muscles, relax your hands and belly, and continuing the circle, slowly lift the chin up as far as you can, separating the muscles of your neck and shoulders. Then slowly jut your chin forward to complete the circle.

Release the tension very slowly, so you are aware of subtle qualities of feeling, and sit quietly for a few minutes, breathing gently, and expanding the sensations in your body. Repeat the movement twice more. Sit for a few minutes after each repetition of the exercise, and for five to ten minutes at the end, sensing and expanding the feelings generated by this movement.

It is important to loosen the neck muscles after doing this exercise. Breathing softly and gently, slowly move your head forward and back, turn it from side to side, and bend it laterally (so your ear moves in the direction of your shoulder). Be sure to do these neck stretches each time you finish the exercise. You may also want to gently massage your neck muscles.

On first glance, this exercise may not seem appealing. It entails performing a motion—jutting out the chin and drawing it back—which may look or sound unattractive. It is also a motion which the body does not ordinarily perform. However, when you try this exercise several times, you may find that it is very effective in releasing tension in the neck area, and that it elicits unusually relaxing feelings. Try it not only during your daily practice, but also during times when you are especially tired or tense.

This exercise releases tension in the neck, head, shoulders, chest, and spine, and equalizes and balances the energies in these areas.

Exercise 46   Refreshing Energy

It is best not to do this exercise if you are pregnant. If you have had a neck or back injury, or an operation within three or four months, do it mindfully.

In this exercise your chin will trace a path similar to two half circles put side by side, somewhat like an 'm'. Sit cross-legged on a mat or cushion, with your hands on your knees. Breathe softly through both nose and mouth. Slowly jut your chin forward, using some strength. Your chest remains straight.

In this position, slowly let your chin draw an arc up and to the right. As your chin approaches your right shoulder, look up to the ceiling. When your chin is over your right shoulder, slowly lower it toward the shoulder, while continuing to look up. Keep your shoulders back a little and loosen your stomach. With your chin still over your shoulder, slowly lift your chin toward the ceiling, and slowly retrace the arc just drawn, moving this time from right to left. When you face straight ahead, slowly arch your chin down toward your chest.

Now without stopping, repeat the above movement, this time to the left side. When you finish, very slowly lift your chin from your chest, releasing the tension and sensing the qualities of feeling stimulated by the exercise. Sit for a few minutes before repeating the exercise.

Do the exercise very slowly three or nine times, sitting briefly after each repetition. At the end, sit for five to ten minutes, allowing the feelings stimulated by this movement to expand.

Afterward, gently loosen the neck muscles in three ways: move your head forward and back, from side to side, and so that your ear moves toward your shoulder. Be sure to do this each time you finish the exercise. Also massage your neck gently if you wish.

Like the preceding exercise, this exercise releases tension in the neck, head, shoulders, chest, and spine, and equalizes the energies in these areas.

Exercise 47   Integrating Body and Mind

It is best not to do this exercise if you are pregnant.
Do it gently if you have had a neck or back injury or
an operation within three or four months.

Sit on a mat or cushion with your legs loosely
crossed so both feet rest on the mat or the floor. Place
your hands on your knees, lift your shoulders a little
and move them back slightly so your arms straighten.

Slowly jut your jaw forward, using some strength, but being sure not to stretch too much. Then, breathing very softly through both nose and mouth, slowly arch your chin down toward your chest. Hold this position for one to three minutes, keeping the breath light and even.

Then slowly lift your chin, and very slowly release the tension in your jaw, shoulders, and neck, sensing the subtle qualities of feeling that arise. Let these feelings be distributed throughout your body.

Rest for a few minutes; then repeat the exercise two more times, resting for several minutes after each repetition, and for five to ten minutes at the end.

Each time you finish the exercise, gently loosen the neck muscles. Slowly move your head forward and back, from side to side, and so that your ear moves toward your shoulder. Also massage your neck gently if you wish.

Like the two preceding exercises, this exercise releases tension in the neck, head, shoulders, chest, and spine, and balances their interconnecting energies.

Exercise 48   Enjoying Space

Stand well balanced with your feet a few inches
apart, your back straight, and your arms relaxed at
your sides. Breathe evenly through both nose and
mouth. Bring your elbows and hands to the level of
your heart, hook your fingers together and pull tensely as if to draw the hands apart. (Your fingernails
must be short!) Move your shoulders back a little.

Facing forward with your eyes soft and still, your feet firmly planted on the ground, and your knees straight but not locked, very slowly twist to the right as far as you can. Take about one minute for this movement. Then very slowly return to the front and without stopping, twist slowly to the left.

Throughout the movement, keep your belly and hips relaxed and your breath easy, while maintaining the tension in your hands, arms, and shoulders. Then slowly return again to the front, and very slowly release the tension, going deeply into the sensations awakened in your body, especially in your spine and shoulders. Slowly lower your arms to your sides, and rest briefly in either a standing or sitting position, continuing to expand the sensations in your body.

Do the complete movement, once to each side, three times, resting for a few minutes after each repetition, and sitting for five to ten minutes at the end.

This exercise can also be done sitting.

Exercise 49   Exercising in Space

Stand with your feet a comfortable distance apart, your back straight, and your body balanced. Breathe lightly and evenly through both nose and mouth. Place your hands on your hips, with as much contact as possible between them. Plant your legs and feet firmly and straighten your knees without locking them.

In this position, very slowly twist only your upper body to the right, moving the head and eyes with the shoulders, arms, and chest. Keep your elbows out and use your hands to help keep the pelvis still by pushing forward on the right hip, and backward on the left hip. Take about thirty seconds for this movement. Then slowly return to the front, again pushing your hands against your hips to keep the pelvis still, and continue turning your upper body to the left.

Your pelvis may move slightly, but if it moves more than a very little, stop and begin again. You may find it helpful to first twist the torso a few times while facing forward, and then add the movement of the head. As you continue to practice the exercise, you will learn to differentiate the turning of the upper body from the turning of the lower body. While the upper body gently exercises, the lower body is steady and rooted, with a strong, concentrative quality. These two qualities give the body a particular kind of balance.

Do the complete movement, to the right and to the left, three or nine times. Then sit in the sitting posture for five minutes, sensing the special character of the energy generated by this movement.

This exercise releases muscular tension in the chest, the upper and middle back, and the neck, and also relaxes the stomach.

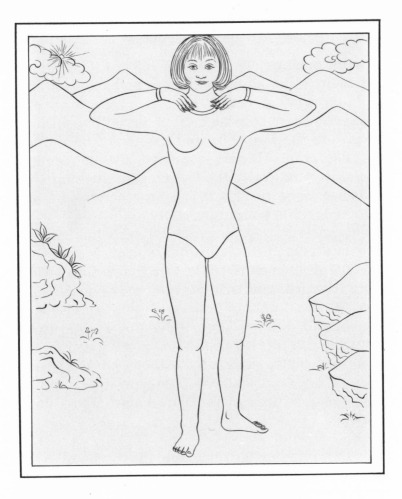

Exercise 50 Interacting Body and Mind

Stand well balanced with your legs a comfortable distance apart, your back straight, and your arms relaxed at your sides. Turn your left foot so the toes point to the left and place your right foot about twelve inches in front of you, with the toes pointing forward, and the heel on a line with the heel of the left foot. Lift your arms away from your sides to shoulder height, and place your hands on your shoulders so the fingers are on the front of the shoulders and the thumbs are on the back. Press with as much contact between hand and shoulder as possible.

In this position, with your eyes open, very slowly begin to rotate your upper torso. Leading with your left elbow, turn your torso to the left as far as you can go without straining, then bend down to the side, letting your head hang. Without stopping, and without raising your torso, continue the rotation to the right, and then slowly straighten up on your right side. As you come up, look toward the ceiling. Then again, leading with your left elbow, slowly turn your torso to the left and begin another rotation. Breathe easily through both nose and mouth throughout, and continue to press your hands against your shoulders.

Do three or nine rotations, very slowly. Then reverse the position of your feet, so the right foot points to the right, and the left foot is about twelve inches in front of you, with the toes pointing forward. In this position, do three or nine very slow rotations, leading the turning of the torso with the right elbow. When you finish, sit in the sitting posture for five to ten minutes, expanding the sensations stimulated by this movement.

This exercise relieves headache, and also relieves tension in the back, shoulders, and legs.

Exercise 51　Touching Alertness

This exercise will be most effective if you have already released tension in your back and neck through massage and some of the exercises in Stage One.

Stand in a well-balanced way with your feet a comfortable distance apart and your back straight. Slowly lift your arms to shoulder height, cross them in front with the elbows at shoulder level, and lightly hold the opposite arm just above the elbow. The arm bones should be well balanced in the shoulder socket, not too far forward or too far back.

Look straight ahead, and thrust your crossed arms twice to the right, beginning the second thrust where the first thrust ends. Exhale through both nose and mouth as fully as possible with each thrust.

With each thrust, increase the distance of the movement until the second thrust brings your arms to the right as far as they can go. Only the arms and shoulders move; the head and torso remain still. You may hear cracking in your middle back, or the back of your neck, as muscles along the spine are adjusted. These movements and breath should have a strong impulse, yet not be shocking or tense. Move easily, in a natural way.

After the thrusts, slowly return your arms to the front, and inhale slowly and fully. Now loosen your shoulders, back muscles, and belly, and do the movement to the left. Do the complete movement, once to the right and once to the left, three times. Then sit in the sitting posture for five minutes or more, following the sensations and feelings quickened in your body.

This exercise relieves tension in the shoulders and the middle back. Through the exhalations, holding in the lower body is also released.

Exercise 52   Vitalizing Energy

Kneel on your right knee with the toes pointing behind you; bend the left knee and place your left foot
on the floor as far in front of you as possible. Place
your right hand on your right hip, and your left hand
on your left knee. Face forward with your back
straight, and in this position, keeping your left foot in
the same place, shift your weight forward and

increase the bend in your left knee until you feel a stretch in both thighs. Make sure your legs are wide apart. Relax your arms, hands, and chest, and hold this position for about thirty seconds, breathing gently through both nose and mouth, and feeling the sensations produced by the stretch.

Then very slowly shift your weight back onto your right leg, slowly straighten your left leg, and slowly flex the left ankle so the toes point to the ceiling. Attend to the subtle qualities of feeling that arise as you do this leg stretch. Then slowly relax the left leg and foot, and kneel on both knees. Rest briefly, continuing to feel the sensations stimulated by the stretches.

Now reverse the position of the legs and hands so you kneel on your left knee and stand on your right foot, with your right hand on your right knee, and your left hand on your left hip. Repeat the exercise in this position.

Do the complete exercise, first on one side, then on the other, three times, resting briefly after each repetition. At the end, sit in the sitting posture for five to ten minutes, expanding the feelings quickened by this exercise.

Exercise 53   Balancing Energy

Stand with your feet a comfortable distance apart. Put your hands behind your back and interlace your fingers so they are on the same side as the palms. As you bend forward slowly from the waist, use your knuckles to massage the big muscles alongside the spine. (This massage can be done through clothes, but is best done directly on the skin.)

Stay down, and let your body be very relaxed as you continue to massage slowly. Be sure to let your head hang loosely from your neck. This massage can be done at different tempos, and with different degrees of pressure. You may wish to start at the lower region of the spine, and slowly rub in one spot until the tension begins to loosen. Then move slowly up the spine, pausing to rub whenever your knuckles touch upon sensitive muscles. Continue up the spine as far as you can reach.

When you finish, relax your arms and rise very slowly, breathing gently, carrying your weight in our legs. Then stand quietly for a few minutes.

This exercise relieves tension, balances the breath, and encourages an even flow of energy throughout the body. It is especially useful after heavy exercise, or after exercising the lower body. Once is usually enough.

Exercise 54   Loosening Up the Self-Image

Stand well balanced with your back straight and
your arms relaxed at your sides. Cross your arms in
front of your chest, the right over the left, and hold
your shoulders with your hands, letting the elbows
hang down. Cross the right leg over the left and place
your right foot next to the left foot. In this position,
breathing gently through both nose and mouth, **very**

slowly bend forward from the waist as low as possible without straining, letting your head hang. Then very slowly rise up and arch backward slightly, concentrating on your feet.

Do the movement three or nine times in this position; then cross the left arm over the right, and the left leg over the right, and repeat the exercise three or nine times. Notice the different qualities of feeling stimulated by the change in position. Then sit in the sitting posture for five to ten minutes, expanding the sensations stimulated by this movement.

If you want to extend this exercise, try it three times with the legs crossed left over right and the arms crossed right over left. Then reverse the position of both arms and legs and repeat three more times. Then sit for five to ten minutes.

☆ As a variation of this exercise, stand with your feet spread wide apart, and cross your arms behind your back, holding your forearms just above the elbows. In this position, very slowly bend forward from the waist, letting your head hang. Very slowly rise and bend backward slightly. Do the movement three or nine times, then sit in the sitting posture for five to ten minutes, expanding the feelings quickened by this version of the movement.

These exercises stimulate the skin and activate new mental and muscular patterns.

Exercise 55   Balancing Mind and Senses

Stand barefoot on the floor or ground with your feet a few inches apart, your back straight, your arms at your sides, and your body balanced. Slowly bend your left knee, clasp it with interlaced hands, draw it up toward your chest, and flex your left ankle so the toes point toward the ceiling. Relax your pelvis, and move your shoulders back a little. Look straight ahead with soft eyes, and balance in this position for one to three minutes, in a relaxed and casual way, breathing gently through both nose and mouth. At first hold your leg tightly with your hands, then slowly release the holding (without moving the leg) until your hands become relaxed. As you do this, keep your chest relaxed.

Now, keeping your hands around your knee, very slowly lower your left leg to the point where you feel control of the movement can pass easily to your leg. Then open your hands gently and casually, and lower your leg to the ground. By sensing the moments at which certain muscles take over a movement, we can learn to combine relaxation and controlled movement. During each phase of this exercise—lifting the leg, holding the position, lowering the leg, and releasing the hands—let your attitude be casual and unambitious. Then you can be sensitive to subtle muscular and energetic changes.

Slowly bring your left foot to the floor, and notice the special feeling-tones that arise just before the foot touches the ground. Continue the exercise, lifting the right knee and balancing on the left leg. Do the complete movement (first one side, then the other) three or nine times, and then sit for five to ten minutes, expanding the feelings quickened by this exercise.

This exercise stimulates several different kinds of energy in the lower body.

Exercise 56   Coordinating Body and Mind

Lie on your right side, your left leg on top of the right,
with your right arm extended overhead on the floor,
palm down. Rest your head on your right arm, and
place your left arm along the side of your body, palm
down. Make sure your body is lying in a straight line.

Keeping your legs straight, flex both ankles so
your toes point toward your head. Slowly stretch

both your left arm and leg as if to lengthen them. Then, continuing the stretch, slowly lift your left arm and leg until the arm is vertical and the leg is as high as it can comfortably go. Keep the ankles flexed. Breathing gently and evenly through both nose and mouth, coordinate this movement so both the arm and leg cover the distance in the same amount of time.

Then, moving as slowly as you can so you feel more, gently lower both your arm and leg, while continuing the stretch. Relax and rest a minute, then repeat the movement two times, resting after each repetition. Then roll onto your left side and do the movement three more times, resting after each repetition.

At the end, roll onto your back, and rest for five to ten minutes. Use the resting time to go deeper into the sensations activated by the movement.

Stage Three

The exercises in this group are a little more difficult than those in the earlier stages. This does not necessarily mean that the movements of the exercises are physically more difficult to do (although some of the movements are more demanding physically than those in earlier exercises). Rather, it means that greater concentration is needed to touch and develop the feeling-tones of the exercises.

After several months of practicing Kum Nye, you will probably find that you are ready for some of these exercises. If you get little result from an exercise, however, put it aside for a while and come back to it later. The exercises toward the end of this stage should be left until you have quite a thorough experience of Kum Nye.

When you have become very familiar with an exercise, (including those in Stage One or Stage Two), try doing it for longer periods of time, perhaps as long as an hour. You might also want to begin experimenting with different tempos and different degrees of tension. Try an exercise slowly; then very slowly; then do it faster, etc. and notice the different qualities of feeling at different speeds. All of the exercises done tensely can also be done 'loosely', and exercises done 'loosely' can also be done tensely. You might also want to try practicing at different times and in different places.

In many of these exercises, a certain position is held for a period of time. (Counting outbreaths will help to measure the time.) Explore the quality of your holding, letting it be as relaxed as possible, without any special purpose. Remember to release the holding very slowly, so that you will feel more, and the sensations quickened by the exercise will last as long as possible. The longer a feeling-tone is expanded, the more it can spread beyond the body, stimulating interactions with surrounding 'space'.

As the feeling expands, bring breath, motion, feeling, and mind into a unity. Balance the breath, balance the senses, balance your awareness, balance your body. Then you develop a quality in your practice that is without holding or clinging, and you discover the joy of exercising without effort.

Exercise 57   Opening the Heart

Sit cross-legged on a mat or cushion, and support
yourself with your right hand on the floor a comfortable distance from you. Make sure your hand is not
too far in front or back. Place your left hand over
your left ear, with the elbow up. In this position,
slowly arch to the right, keeping your right arm
straight. Support yourself well with your right hand

so the arching of your left side can be both maximized and balanced. Keep your knees down as much as possible. Let your ribs lift away from your pelvis, and open like a fan all the way to the underarm; let space expand within the bones of your hip and ribs, and in the muscles under your arm. Hold this position for one to three minutes, breathing softly and evenly through nose and mouth.

Release the stretch very slowly—take about one minute for this—feeling the sensations generated by holding this position. Then place your right hand over your right ear, support yourself with your left hand on the floor beside you, and arch slowly to the left. Do the complete exercise (first one side and then the other) three or nine times, then sit quietly in the sitting posture for five to ten minutes and taste the quality of this feeling of relaxation.

This exercise opens the heart center, improves breathing and circulation, and massages internal muscles.

Exercise 58   Coordinating the Wholeness of Energy

Stand barefoot with your back straight, your feet wide apart and pointed straight ahead, and your hands on your hips. Your body and mind should be well balanced and concentrated. Turn your right foot to the right until it is at a right angle to your left foot, bend your right knee, and turn your torso to the right so you face the same direction as your right foot. Keep your left leg and your back straight. Look at a spot on the wall in front of you near the ceiling, with your head back, your chin in, your chest high, and your elbows out. Relax your belly and breathe smoothly through both nose and mouth.

In this position, lower your body by increasing the bend in your right knee and relaxing your pelvis. As you move down, keep your back and your left leg straight. Lower until you reach a place of both tension and energy. Do not worry if you are unable to find this place immediately; see how you feel at different points as you go down, and let your feelings guide you to the place where sensation is strongest.

When you find this place, hold until you begin to shake; then return very slowly to an upright position. Turn your right toes and torso to the left so you again face forward, and move your feet closer together. Move slowly and keep in contact with your feelings throughout the movement. Breathe softly and evenly so that all of the different steps involved in the exercise can flow smoothly and easily into each other.

If you find holding difficult to do at first, move down and up slowly several times until you become more familiar with the sensation of tension in the right knee and leg. Then try holding the position for a few seconds.

Now slowly change the position of your feet so that your left foot points to the left and is at a right angle to your right foot. Continue the exercise on the left side. As you move, always take care to keep the movements flowing smoothly. Keep in touch with your feelings; do not let the movement become mechanical. Do the complete exercise, including both sides, three times, then sit in the sitting posture for five to ten minutes, expanding the feelings generated by this movement.

When you have practiced the above exercise ten times over a period of at least a week, try these variations.

☆   Coordinate your breathing with the exercise described above by slowly exhaling as you turn to the right and lower your body, and inhaling as you rise and return to the front. Exhale again slowly as you continue the exercise to the left. Do the motion very slowly and with concentration. There is one slow continuous stretch-motion and breath.

Always remain balanced. If you feel at any moment that you might lose control of the movement, then slowly bring your feet together and begin again with your legs a little closer together. Do the complete movement (to both right and left) three times; then sit for five to ten mintues, expanding your feelings. Through this exercise you can explore with clarity the interconnections among body, breath, and mind.

☆   Lower your body to the position described above, with your right foot turned to the right, at a right angle to your left foot, your right knee bent, your head and torso facing right, and your hands on your hips. Hold briefly, breathing very gently through both nose and mouth. Then without returning to an upright position, very slowly rotate to the left—first turning your head to the left, then your shoulders, chest, pelvis, and feet. At the end of the rotation, your left foot will point to the left at a right angle to your right foot, and your head and torso will face the same direction as your left foot.

The rotation should be done extremely slowly, with a clear sense of controlling the movement. Be sure not to stretch too much. Continue the exercise without returning to an upright position until you have done the complete movement (to both right and left) three times. Then slowly bring your feet together, and sit in the sitting posture for ten minutes, expanding the energies generated by the exercise.

These exercises increase coordination. They develop the muscles of the legs, and stimulate the flow of energy from the legs, through the back, to the head.

Exercise 59   Transforming Emotions

Stand well balanced with your feet close together
and your back straight. Cross your arms in front of
your chest and hold your shoulders with your hands,
your elbows down. With your legs together and your
heels on the floor, slowly bend at the knees with your
back straight, as if sitting down in a low chair. Maintain internal balance as you lower, without tensing

up. When you have gone down a certain distance in this position, you may find that tightness somewhere prevents you from going further, and you are beginning to lift your heels from the floor. Stop and locate the tension—it may be in your pelvis or legs. Let it go, and continue to lower, keeping your back straight.

Well above a squatting position you will discover a special place of balance and energy. You may need to move up and down a little until you find the right place. You may feel heat rise in your body, and you may begin to shake. You will feel pressure on your knees. Stay with these sensations, and hold this position for one to five minutes, with your chin in and your back straight, concentrating on the energy in your spine.

Then very slowly return to a standing position, releasing the tension. Stand silently with your arms at your sides for three to five minutes; then repeat the exercise twice, standing or sitting quietly after each repetition. Now sit in the sitting posture for ten to fifteen minutes, expanding the sensations generated by this movement.

The close connections among our bodies, senses, and emotions allow us to affect our whole state of balance through a physical posture. Usually our emotions throw us off balance. In this exercise, we can transform strong emotion such as resentment or anxiety, using the energy of the emotion to keep us balanced, rather than dissipating it through negativity. If you hold the position long enough, pure energy will flow throughout your body.

As you do the exercise, search out the inner tensions which throw you off balance, and release them. Feel for any memory which makes you tense, and relax it so that it flows like liquid. Breathe softly and gently into places of blockage. Even if an emotion is so strong that the holding manifests as pain, breathe into the pain until the holding relaxes and you discover a kernel of new energy. Keep your belly relaxed so that energy rising up from the legs can flow through your spine and be distributed to your whole body. Close your eyes and go inside for your inner balance. With practice, the exercise may become effortless.

This exercise stimulates all energies in the lower body, helps to stimulate hormones, and increases circulation.

Exercise 60   Relieving Negativity

Stand well balanced with your feet a comfortable
distance apart, your back straight, and your arms
relaxed at your sides. Bend your elbows and place
your hands flat against the sides of your body, as
close under the armpits as possible, with the fingers
pointing straight down. This may be a little difficult
to do at first, and you may need to experiment to find

the easiest way to do it. Do not press your sides too hard.

Breathing softly through both nose and mouth, bend your knees, and with your heels on the floor and your back straight, lower your body as if sitting down in a low chair. When you have lowered a certain distance, you may find that tension somewhere prevents you from going further, and your heels may begin to lift from the floor. Stop and locate the tension. Then let it go, and continue to lower with your back straight until you find a specific point of balance and energy. You may need to move up and down a little until you find the right place. (If you have done Exercise 59, you have already found it.) Your thighs may begin to shake.

When you find the place, look up, and hold this position for thirty seconds to one minute. If you feel pain in your arms, go into the sensations of pain as fully as you can. Then slowly straighten your legs, and in a continuing movement, bend forward at the waist to about waist level, and hold briefly, keeping your breathing slow and gentle. Then without changing the rest of the position, slowly bend your knees until you reach the special point of balance and energy, and when your legs begin to shake, hold for thirty seconds to one minute, breathing softly through nose and mouth. You may feel sensations of energy at the base of the spine as well as in the thighs.

Now slowly straighten your legs, raise your torso, and let your hands slide down your sides until your arms hang relaxed at your sides. Stand or sit for a few minutes, expanding the feelings generated by this exercise.

Do the exercise three times, resting after each repetition. To complete it, sit in the sitting posture for five to ten minutes, continuing to expand the feelings within and around your body.

As you do this exercise, you may feel some painful sensations at first. Customarily we think of pain as something to be avoided. Yet if you can concentrate on the sensations which are produced by this exercise (and by other exercises which involve holding a position for a period of time), you can go beyond the mental concept of 'pain' to a source of new and vital energy.

As you concentrate, let your breathing merge with your sensations and transform them into healing energy. If you wish, hold the position mentioned in the exercise for just a few seconds at first. When you have had more experience with tapping the energy held within tension, you will be able to hold this position for several minutes or more.

This exercise energizes the lower body and chest, relieves negative psychological patterns such as holding back, and builds strength and confidence.

Exercise 61   Expanding Body Energy

Stand well balanced with your feet a few inches apart and your arms relaxed at your sides. Make tight fists with both hands. Extend your left arm in front of you at shoulder height. Raise your right arm to shoulder height, bend it at the elbow, and place the right fist under the left arm, just above the elbow joint; the top of the fist (the thumb and index finger) will touch the underside of the left arm. Make sure the right elbow is at shoulder height.

Create strong opposing forces by pushing down with the left arm and up with the right. Maintain both strong tension and balance, and while inhaling through both nose and mouth, slowly raise both arms until the left arm is vertical and the right arm is bent over the head. The right arm should clear the head; if it does not, stretch the arms up slightly.

In this position, continuing to maintain the tension in the arms, exhale slowly, relaxing your belly, neck, and back. Then slowly lower your arms to shoulder height while inhaling, and as you do so, slowly release the tension in your arms. Let your breathing be smooth and easy throughout the movement. Lower your arms to your sides and rest for a minute, either standing or sitting, expanding the sensations produced by creating and releasing tension in this way.

Now reverse the position of the arms and repeat the movement, resting briefly afterward. Do the complete movement (once on each side) three times, resting after each side. At the end, sit in the sitting posture for five to ten minutes, continuing to expand the feelings stimulated by this movement.

This exercise, which can also be done sitting, relieves muscular tension, improves the circulation, and balances inner energies.

Exercise 62   Increasing Endurance

Stand barefoot and balance on your right leg with the sole of your left foot pressed against your upper right thigh, the heel near the crotch, and the left knee out to the side. Lightly press the heel against the thigh to help keep the left foot in place. Without effort, slowly lift your arms away from your sides, letting them float up until they are extended at slightly above shoulder height, with the palms down.

In this position, slowly turn at the waist to the right, and then to the left, keeping your head still and looking straight ahead with soft eyes. Move casually, breathing lightly and evenly, with your body loose and almost sleepy, and your belly relaxed. Let the pressure of your left foot against your right thigh be as light as possible.

Then slowly lower your arms and leg at the same time, sensing the subtle changes in feeling as you come to balance again on both feet. Stand quietly for a minute. You may feel a release of tension in the neck and shoulders and a balanced feeling throughout your torso.

Now reverse the position of the legs, and repeat the movement. Do the complete movement, balancing first on one leg, then the other, three or nine times, standing briefly on both feet after each repetition. At the end, sit for five to ten minutes, expanding the feelings stimulated by the exercise.

This exercise balances body energy, and develops the ability to stay balanced during critical points of emotional or psychological change.

Exercise 63　Embracing Space

Stand barefoot and balance on your right leg with the
sole of your left foot pressed against your upper right
thigh, and your left knee out to the side. Slowly lift
your arms in front of you to shoulder height and then
cross them, holding the arms tightly just above the
elbow. Slowly raise your arms over and a little behind your head, stretching upward. Let your neck

settle down between your shoulders. Slowly look toward the ceiling, open your mouth, and stretch a little more. Balance casually in this position. Loosen your belly; you may then find you can stretch a little more. Your upper back may be slightly arched.

Now slowly unfold your arms, with the palms toward the ceiling, until your arms straighten overhead. In a slow, uninterrupted motion, lower your arms to your sides, as if drawing angel wings in snow. Allow your hands and chest to open. When your arms reach your sides, slowly lower your leg to the floor, until you are standing on both feet. Notice the special flavors of feeling that come just before your foot touches the floor.

Now slowly reverse the position of your legs and repeat the movement. This time inhale slowly as you stretch your tightly crossed arms upward. Hold the inhalation for a few seconds, with your arms overhead; then begin to exhale slowly as you open your arms upward, and continue to exhale as your arms slowly float down to your sides. Your arm gesture can be very generous and expressive, opening the chest, and embracing space. Let this movement of your arms be extremely slow and gentle.

Do the complete movement (first one side and then the other) three times, coordinating your breathing with the movement. When you finish, stand silently on both feet for several minutes, your arms relaxed at your sides; then sit for five to ten minutes. You may feel a deep calm within your bones, especially the bones of your arms and chest.

This exercise may also be done standing on both legs, or sitting.

Exercise 64   Increasing Psychological Balance

Stand barefoot, and balance on your left leg with the sole of your right foot against your upper left thigh and your right knee out to the side. Slowly extend your right arm in front of you at shoulder height, palm down. Place the left palm on top of the right elbow, with your left elbow at shoulder height. Push your right arm up toward the ceiling while strongly resisting this movement with your left arm. As you do this, relax your belly as much as possible, and breathe evenly and softly through both nose and mouth. When both arms are overhead, slowly release the tension and lower your arms to the first position, sensing the feelings that arise in and around your body.

Do the movement three times; then reverse the position of your legs and arms and do the exercise three times on the other side. At the end, sit in the sitting posture for five to ten minutes, following and expanding the feelings generated by this exercise.

This exercise is very calming to the nervous system. However, if you practice it when you are nervous or upset, you may need to begin the 'balancing process' by sitting quietly for ten or fifteen minutes, breathing gently and evenly through both nose and mouth. When you begin the exercise, move very slowly, bringing breath, awareness, and motion into a unity. The exercise will then continue to calm and balance your mind and body.

Exercise 65 Sameness of Inner and Outer

Stand barefoot on the floor, well balanced, with your back straight and your hands on your hips. Slowly bend your left knee and raise it toward your chest. Flex your left ankle so the toes point to the ceiling (the foot stays in this position throughout the movement). With your back straight and your belly relaxed, slowly straighten your left leg in front of you, with a slight kick at the very end of the stretch, and at the same time, push your chest forward a little. When straight, the leg is as nearly horizontal as possible. Then without putting the foot down, twice more draw your leg up toward your chest and slowly straighten it. The movement has the quality of slow leg stretches.

After three leg stretches, very slowly, almost casually, lower your left leg to the floor. Notice any special flavors of feeling that come just before your foot meets the ground.

Now slowly lift your right knee and do the exercise on the other side. Without effort, maintain control of the movement throughout, keeping it smooth and slow. Watch the tension in your belly to gauge your level of anxiety. When you tighten your belly in order to exert control, you lose touch with precious energies which bring vitality. If you can be casual at critical points in the movement without forcing control, you will discover certain vital qualities and energies.

Do the complete movement, first on one side and then on the other, three times, and then sit for five to ten minutes, following and extending the feelings stimulated by this exercise. When you are familiar with the exercise, try it nine times, sitting for five to ten minutes after each set of three movements.

This exercise improves coordination, increases body energy, and relieves tension in the chest.

Exercise 66 Increasing Inner Balance

Lie on your right side with your legs straight, the left leg on top of the right. Interlace your fingers and place them behind your head so that your head rests on your right arm and your left elbow points to the ceiling. In this position, slowly begin to stretch, moving your left hip toward the floor in front of you, and at the same time, moving your left elbow to the left until you look up at the ceiling and your left shoulder comes near the floor. Notice that as your hip moves forward, your legs may turn so that you can stand on your toes. Although it is possible to stretch until the lower half of the body faces the floor and the upper half faces the ceiling, do not be concerned if you do not stretch this far. Move easily, without straining; it does not matter how far you stretch.

Hold the stretch for thirty seconds to a minute, breathing softly through both nose and mouth, and gently increasing the stretch as subtle tensions are released. Then slowly return to the original position, expanding the sensations awakened by this stretch.

Now roll onto your left side, and repeat the stretch. Notice on which side of your body the stretch is easier. Do the complete exercise, to the right and left, three times. Then rest on your back (with your knees bent if you wish) for five minutes, continuing to expand the sensations stimulated by the exercise.

This exercise gives inner balance to both the upper and lower body.

Stimulating and Transforming Energies

The body is like a vessel
filled and surrounded by space.
The whole body exercises in space.

Energy is continuously being channeled through our bodies, from cell to cell, between our minds and our bodies, as well as between ourselves and the world around us. As we move and experience, even as we breathe, the energies within and around us continuously interact. We tend to think of energy and matter as being opposites, but even the most solid objects are actually made up of moving energies: matter and energy are, on all levels, equivalent. Our physical bodies are much less solid than they seem. They are not fixed and impervious 'objects', but are essentially flowing and open, participating in an on-going process of 'embodiment' of energies.

When these energies flow smoothly, we have access to all the energy we could hope for. The body becomes healthy, and the mind clear. When this flow of energy is active and balanced, it regenerates every aspect of our bodies, minds, and senses, continuously increasing our mental and physical vitality. Feelings of love and openness nourish and renew us, radiating to the surrounding environment. All our experience participates in this ongoing process of enjoyment and embodiment.

When we prevent this completely open flow, slowing the energies down and misdirecting them, our experience becomes contracted. We mentally freeze our sensations by concentrating on our thoughts *about* them, instead of experiencing our sensations directly, letting them flow to our hearts where they deepen into nourishing joy and satisfaction. We become like bees, tapping beautiful flowers for pollen, but never enjoying the honey.

Looking for sensation and satisfaction, we direct our energies outwards. We fill our minds with ideas and expectations of what we want for the future, instead of enjoying what is at hand. We skim over the surface of our feelings. In order to 'feel more' we may direct our energy into our emotions, which quickly and easily feed us strong sensations. But these sensations are imbalanced, and cannot truly satisfy us —they stir up dissatisfaction instead of fulfillment. Psychological tensions then manifest on the physical level, automatically producing more tightening, which is reflected in negative patterns of thought, feeling, and action.

Our ability to contact our senses diminishes, so our vitality also decreases. In reaction we may try to 'save our energy' by relying on external forms of energy rather than our own, but this only continues to undermine both our vitality and our health. We then try to heal ourselves, taking our bodies to one place and our heads to another, not realizing that the remedy for both is in the naturally wholesome energies of our sensations and feelings, and in the integration of our bodies and minds.

Relaxation can heal both body and mind by awakening our inner resources, opening us to feelings which are much more than physical or even mental sensations. Our ordinary feelings and sensations are of several different kinds, some relating to our body awareness, others relating to our sensory or mental awareness. During relaxation, interactions are stimulated among body, senses, breath, and mind which bring these different kinds of awareness and feeling into contact with each other.

As they expand and accumulate, these feelings and energies flow together and become integrated; once integrated, they naturally stimulate each other, developing further within themselves. Then every sense impression, breath, and movement increases and deepens enjoyment, and experience comes alive in the body. A deep feeling of fulfillment flows through every vein and organ, gathering richness until the boundaries within the body dissolve and the very outline of the body melts into surrounding space. Then living becomes enjoyment, and stimulation becomes relaxation. The texture of space nourishes us.

When we discover the fulfilling intimacy of direct experience, we see that everything that arises, every feeling and sensation, is a center of experience. We do not do or accomplish anything, for there is no experiencer; there is only experience. This knowledge gives us the possibility of new interactions with 'negative' emotions such as confusion or resistance, for we see that they too are flexible forms of vital energy and experience which can open into positive directions.

As you practice the exercises in this section, go deeply into the feelings generated, bringing body, mind, and senses together. Expand your sensations, letting them become vital and strong. As 'breath' and subtle mental and physical energies become integrated, these sensations become much deeper and more expansive than our ordinary sensations. As these feelings are channeled through our senses, all of our sensations and feelings become vibrant and alive, much richer than before. Our whole body grows saturated with this quality of joyful vitality and becomes wholesome: a body of knowledge.

When you touch a negative emotion or a tight place in your body or mind, let these sleeping energies awaken. Mix them with your rich and joyful sensations, balance your breath, and keep your awareness open, without focusing too strongly. Stay with the feelings; let them become exhilarating, and penetrate them with awareness and breath. With enough concentration, you can actually transform these feelings by a process of inner alchemy.

As you practice Kum Nye, you may experience an energy center opening. When the head center opens it becomes easy to think and communicate clearly, and visionary powers become possible. Intuitive powers develop when the throat center opens, revealing to us the symbolic world of poetry and art. When the heart center opens, separation between ourselves and others dissolves, and we become a part of everything. Craving and grasping cease when the navel center opens, and a quality of energy like heat warms the whole body.

Once we learn to stimulate our feelings and energies through the practice of Kum Nye, we can expand them more and more each day, cultivating enjoyment and playfulness in every action. We can even enjoy stressful situations because we can replenish our energy whenever we grow tired. Everything we do gives us more energy. Directed like the point of a bright beam, each moment of life kindles accomplishment, enabling us to develop genuine perseverance and patience, without struggle or fixation. Then we can naturally do and simultaneously enjoy all the content of experience. We can fully appreciate the process of living within our 'body of knowledge' so that all mental and physical experience of living automatically continues to expand. Experience just opens of itself, naturally.

Without trying to possess them, we can let feelings of enjoyment stream through us and outside us, stimulating harmonious interactions in the world around us. Anything we contact, through sound, touch, or any of the senses, becomes radiant with subtle energy. Even walking or looking in a relaxed, open way allows the special light quality of universal energies to enter our bodies; then we can cultivate and expand that feeling until it permeates our bodies and spreads out from us into the universe. In this way we participate in a continuous circle of living energies, a dance of appreciation, a commingling.

Stage One

Like the exercises in "Balancing and Integrating Body, Mind, and Senses," these exercises are divided into three stages in order of difficulty. Each stage is equivalent to the corresponding stage in the previous chapter. You may want to move back and forth between chapters in exploring the exercises at a given stage.

You may also want to explore some of the exercises in Stages Two and Three before completing all of the exercises in the first stage. Let your body and your feelings guide you in selecting exercises to practice. However, if you find that you are racing through the exercises without going deeply into any of them, slow down and follow the progression of exercises given here. Remember to do each exercise completely, either three or nine times, and when it is appropriate, on both sides of the body.

Each exercise, no matter how simple on the surface, can unlock the treasure-house of experience in your body and mind. During the exercise, it is best not to be concerned with whether your feeling is good or bad—just feel it. Do not let the feelings mentioned in the exercise descriptions create expectations you feel you must meet in order to 'succeed' at the exercise. Simply tune your sensations, tune your breath, tune your awareness; then, although you may think 'nothing special' is happening, Kum Nye will naturally vitalize even the most subtle layers of your body, mind, and senses. After practicing, observe the quality of your experience during the day. Even in a short time you will notice a more vibrant quality to daily life and your capacity for enjoyment will increase.

The exercises in this stage are all simple to do. Do them slowly, with sensitive attention to the sensations that occur throughout your whole body. Exercise 72, in particular, when practiced regularly over a period of at least one week, will greatly increase your awareness of the energy 'centers'. As these centers become more open, and internal organs and muscles are deeply massaged, a warm, gentle, deeply satisfying feeling begins to nurture and sustain you. As this process deepens, this harmonious feeling nurtures those around you as well.

Exercise 67 Sensing Energy

Sit cross-legged on a mat or cushion and slowly extend your arms in front of you at shoulder height,
palms down. Keeping your belly relaxed, move your
hands back by pulling your shoulders back; then
reach forward with your hands. Very slowly move
your arms back and forth in this way nine times. The
rest of your body remains still. Let the motion and

your mind become inseparable. Then slowly find a place of balance in the shoulder sockets, neither forward nor back, and lower your hands to your knees. Sit for three to five minutes, allowing the feelings and currents of energy stimulated by this movement to expand.

Now again extend your arms in front of you, and slowly bend your arms at the elbow until your fingers point to the ceiling. Relax your neck as you do this movement. Then very slowly lower your forearms until your arms are outstretched in front of you. Your upper arms remain still as your forearms move down very subtly. Feel the energy in your chest, within your heart center; there may be a feeling there of something moving down. Put your entire consciousness into whatever you feel; the feeling then becomes consciousness. Do this movement nine times, breathing softly and evenly through both nose and mouth; then slowly lower your hands to your knees and sit for five to ten minutes.

Exercise 68   Clearing Confusion

Sit on a rug or a flat mat and cross your legs in the manner illustrated in the drawing. Take hold of your right ankle with your right hand and your left ankle with your left hand, and draw your feet along the floor as close to your body as you can. Then place your hands just below the kneecaps and draw your knees as close as possible toward your chest, keeping your back straight and your shoulders down. If possible, touch your knees to your chest. Look straight ahead and hold for one to three minutes, breathing softly through both nose and mouth, and concentrating lightly on your belly. (Count outbreaths to measure time if you wish.)

Now very slowly release the tension—take about one minute for this—feeling the sensations that arise in your body. Sit quietly in the sitting posture for a few minutes, continuing to explore these sensations. Then repeat the exercise, reversing the position of the legs as you cross them. Do the exercise three or nine times, sitting for a few minutes after each repetition, and for five to ten minutes at the end.

This exercise energizes the navel center, and clears confusion from the mind.

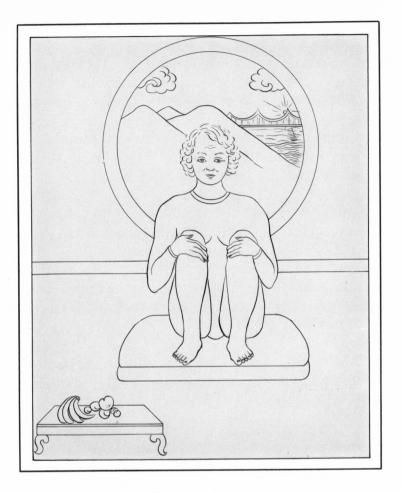

Exercise 69 Clear Mind

This exercise differs from the preceding exercise in the position of the legs. Sit on a rug or flat mat with your knees bent and your feet flat on the floor in front of you. Take hold of the left ankle with your left hand and the right ankle with your right hand. Draw your feet along the floor as close to your body as you can. Then place your hands just below the kneecaps and draw your knees as close to your chest as possible, keeping your back straight and your shoulders down. If possible, touch your knees to your chest. Look straight ahead and hold for one to three minutes, breathing softly through both nose and mouth, and concentrating lightly on your belly. (Count out-breaths to measure time if you wish.)

Now very slowly release the tension—take about one minute for this—going deeply into the sensations stimulated in your body. Sit quietly in the sitting posture for a few minutes, continuing to expand these sensations. Do the exercise three or nine times, sitting for a few minutes after each repetition, and for five to ten minutes at the end.

This exercise, like the preceding exercise, increases energy in the lower energy center, and brings clarity to the mind.

Exercise 70　Light Energy

Do this exercise very gently if you are pregnant or have had any neck or back injuries, or if you have had an operation within the last three or four months.

Sit on the floor (not on a mat or cushion) with your legs loosely crossed, the left leg outside of the right. Raise your left knee and bring your left heel in front of your right ankle, with the sole of your left foot on the floor. Interlace your fingers and clasp your left knee with your hands. Very gradually arch your spine and neck backwards. Do not let your head go all the way back; the curve in the spine is graceful and not extreme. To strengthen the arch, gently pull on your knee. Keep your right knee on the floor if you can. Do not stretch too strenuously. Hold the stretch for three to five minutes, breathing gently and evenly through both nose and mouth. Concentrate lightly on energy moving up your spine.

When you feel heat at the back of your neck, very slowly release the tension. Take at least a minute to straighten your spine, expanding feelings of warmth and energy. Do the exercise three times on one side; then reverse the position of the legs and do the exercise three times on the other side. Sit quietly for ten minutes at the conclusion of the exercise, allowing the feelings stimulated by the movement to radiate like a halo.

This exercise releases tension in the spine.

Exercise 71 Releasing Tension

Sit on a mat or cushion with your legs loosely
crossed, the left leg outside the right. Raise your left
knee and bring your left heel in front of your right
ankle, with the sole of your left foot flat on the floor or
mat. Draw your feet as close to your body as you can,
and place your hands on your knees.

Now very slowly and gently stretch your neck

back and to the left, so that your right arm straightens and your head and neck come into a line with your right arm. Keep the right knee down. Hold the diagonal stretch for about thirty seconds, breathing gently and evenly through both nose and mouth.

Then release the tension very slowly, taking thirty seconds to one minute to do so. Let your breath and awareness flow with the sensations awakened in your body. Sit quietly for a few minutes, allowing these sensations to expand. Then reverse the position of your legs, and stretch your neck toward the other side. Rest briefly afterward.

Do the complete exercise, first on one side, then the other, three or nine times, resting for a few minutes after each side. Be sure to release the tension very slowly. At the end of the exercise, sit in the sitting posture for five to ten minutes, continuing to expand the sensations generated by the stretch.

This exercise releases tension in the neck, shoulders, and head; it can relieve headache.

Exercise 72   Embodiment

Sit comfortably in the sitting posture. Concentrate on
the energy center below the navel for half an hour a
day for three days. Breathe gently and evenly through
both nose and mouth, and keep your eyes half-open if
possible. Sometimes it is easier in the beginning to
close the eyes, and this is also all right. Begin by doing
whatever you do when you concentrate. After two

days, change the quality of the concentration so it becomes less forceful, and there is simply a quality of awareness. With this kind of concentration, your body energy will flow: calm feelings arise gradually, and thoughts slow down.

At times the feeling is soft and gentle, like warm milk, very thick, rich, and deep. Become very still, and expand the feelings; this will make them last longer. Feel them as much as you can, and send them to all the different parts of your body—up to your face and neck, and down to your feet and toes. Subtly hold the breath, just a little tightly, in the lower part of the belly and in the sacrum; then expand the feelings to your whole body, more and more, until it is as if the whole universe were to become those feelings. The feelings blow like a warm summer breeze in a hot place, healing you within and without, passing through many layers of your body: first your skin, in and between the surface tissues and nerves; then deeper within, to nerves, tissues, and organs. Sometimes the feelings move deep within like a little whirl of wind.

After you have concentrated on the navel center in this way for half an hour a day for three days, move to the heart center and concentrate there for an equal amount of time. Then move to the throat center, and finally, to the head center between the eyes.

If you want to try concentrating in this way for a longer period of time, concentrate on each energy center for half an hour a day for two or three weeks. Then certain experiences may occur. Colors—perhaps green or white light, or red, orange, blue, or mixed colors—may appear. You may see different objects, or feel various feeling-tones, or hear a very high-pitched sound. If any of these or other experiences occur, do not become attached or fascinated by them. Simply allow them to happen, and expand the sensations as much as you can.

If too many thoughts make it difficult for you to sleep, lightly concentrate on the heart center for half an hour every evening for two weeks. Try not to think about anything; do not read or write after the exercise. Just go into the feeling in your heart center, deepening and expanding it until a joyful quality develops. Continue it, more and more, as if there were nothing else in the world, only this feeling.

Exercise 73 OM AH HUM

Sit in the sitting posture on a mat or cushion. Breathe
softly through both nose and mouth. Think of the
mantra OM AH HUM, feeling OM in the head center at
the top of the head, AH in the throat center, and HUM
in the heart center. Begin to chant the mantra inwardly, quite slowly.

Now silently chant OM with your hands on your

knees. Then slowly move your hands in front of your belly with the palms up, and cradle the fingers of the right hand in the fingers of the left hand. Lift the thumbs a little and join them, as in the drawing. In this position, inwardly chant AH. Then slowly move your hands, palms up, to your knees, and rest them there, silently chanting HUM. Begin a new cycle by turning your hands over on your knees while chanting OM.

Continue in this way for twenty-five complete cycles, combining your inward chanting of the mantra with the movement. Let breath, chant, and movement become one. When you finish, sit quietly in the sitting posture for five to ten minutes, expanding the sensations awakened by this exercise. Throughout the day, silently remember OM AH HUM from time to time.

Exercise 74 Wholesome Vitality

Stand well balanced with your back straight, your arms relaxed at your sides, and your feet a comfortable distance apart, with the toes turned out slightly. Bend your elbows and place your hands flat against the sides of the body, as close under the armpits as possible, with the fingers pointing straight down. This may be a little hard to do at first. Do not press

your sides too hard. Inhale deeply through both nose
and mouth, then gently and silently hold the breath,
and concentrate lightly on your chest. Relax your
belly and tighten the buttocks a little. Then while still
holding the breath, bend your knees slightly and
hold. If you feel pain in your arms, go into the sensations as deeply as you can.

Now slowly exhale, and at the same time straight-
en your legs and glide your hands down the sides of
the body until your arms hang relaxed at your sides.
Let the contact between your hands and body be
as full as possible as you do this. Stand or sit for a
few minutes, breathing gently through both nose and
mouth, expanding the sensations in your body. You
may feel heat in your chest and the back of your neck.

Do the exercise three times, standing or sitting
briefly after each repetition. At the end, sit in the
sitting posture for five to ten minutes, continuing to
expand the feelings produced by this exercise. Your
head may feel clearer, your heart more open, and
your senses more alive.

Exercise 75 Body of Energy

Lie on your back with your arms at your sides, and
your legs separated about the width of your pelvis.
Bend your knees, one at a time, and place your feet
flat on the floor. With the palms facing each other,
slowly lift your arms to the ceiling. In this position,
roll your pelvis and knees toward your chest, lifting
them as high off the floor as possible. The back of

your waistline will come off the floor, and your arms will move apart a little. Keeping your arms up, slowly roll back until your pelvis and feet rest on the floor. Breathe easily through both nose and mouth throughout the movement. Continue three times, expanding the sensations awakened by the roll.

Now do the movement quickly, six to nine times, breathing gently through both nose and mouth. Then straighten your legs one at a time, lower your arms to your sides and rest on your back for a few minutes, continuing to amplify and extend the feelings in and around your body.

Do the exercise three times (beginning with three slow rolls, then six to nine quick rolls), resting on your back after each repetition and at the end of the whole series.

This exercise releases tension from the muscles of the lower abdomen, relieves emotions, and refreshes the whole body.

Stage Two

These exercises activate energies in many specific areas of the body, including the hands, wrists, arms, chest, shoulders, back, thighs, legs, and toes. As you do them, distribute the sensations awakened in a particular place until your whole body participates in the 'massage'. You will find that the exercises which lengthen the muscles along the spine release particularly joyful sensations.

When an exercise involves a stretch, slowly ease into the stretch, breathing softly and evenly, developing a quality of lightness. Be sure not to stretch too much. Remember to 'hold' a position lightly too, breathing gently and releasing subtle tensions throughout your body. If you wish, use your breath to measure time by counting outbreaths. Release holding or tension very slowly, maintaining the quality of lightness, and allowing your sensations to expand.

When you notice a tight place in your body and mind, explore it, without dwelling on it. If you wish, use the tension as 'food' for Exercises 87 and 89. With continuing practice of Kum Nye, the tension will gradually melt, stimulating energy to flow evenly throughout your body until it cycles and recycles, constantly replenishing itself.

Exercise 76   Building Strength and Confidence

Sit cross-legged on a mat or cushion, and press your
palms together with the fingers pointing straight
ahead; then press the heels of your hands into the
center of your chest. Keeping your palms pressed
tightly together, separate your fingers and thumbs
from each other, and slowly and steadily move them
apart and back as much as possible, with your elbows

out and your shoulders down. Be sure to press the palms together as you do this, and relax your belly. The back of your neck will be a little stiff. Breathing softly through both nose and mouth, hold this position for three minutes, until your palms become heated. Then very slowly release the tension, feeling the sensations that arise.

Now do the exercise again, holding the position this time for five minutes, separating your fingers and thumbs as much as possible. After five minutes, release the tension slowly and bring your hands to your eyes, cupping them over your open eyes so that no light shines through. (Do not actually touch your eyes.) Look softly, slowly opening to the inside of the energy. Can you feel something? There may be a sensation of warmth or flowing energy.

Now stare strongly into the dark cave made by your hands, breathing softly and evenly through both nose and mouth. Once you have heated up the palms, you can stare for as long as ten minutes. You may see tiny stars, vibrations, colors, light or darkness, or have very pleasurable feelings. After five to ten minutes, slowly lower your hands to your knees, and look around you slowly and gently. What do you feel? Is there a special quality or sensation to your seeing?

You can also bring your palms, once they are heated, to many other parts of your body. Try the following two suggestions, and then experiment on your own.

☆ Heat up your palms again, holding for five minutes, then put one hand crosswise on your chest and
the other crosswise on the middle of your back. Let
the whole hand come in contact with your body. Feel
the warmth penetrate your chest and spine, as if you
had no skin. After a few minutes, bring one hand to
your forehead and the other to the back of your head,
and continue to sense the feelings in your body.

Exercise 77　Stream of Energy

Sit cross-legged on a mat or cushion with your back
straight. Lightly press your elbows to your sides, and
lift your forearms in front of you until they are
roughly parallel to the floor, with the palms down.
Breathing evenly through both nose and mouth, lift
your shoulders slightly and hold, with your chest
relaxed. Keeping the fingers and thumb of each hand

together, slowly bend your wrists so your fingers point toward the floor. There is an arching quality to this bending. Hold the hands down for one minute, with the rest of the body still and relaxed. Then very slowly lift your hands, releasing the tension and sensing the feelings stimulated in your hands, arms, chest, and the back of your neck. You may feel energy flowing through your wrists and arms to your heart center and spine. Allow whatever sensations you feel to expand.

Lower your hands to your knees and rest briefly. Then repeat the movement, this time increasing the bend in the wrist so your hands come closer to the underside of your forearm. Hold for one to five minutes before slowly releasing the tension.

Do the movement three or nine times, resting briefly after each repetition. At the end, sit for five to ten minutes, expanding and distributing your sensations throughout your body, and beyond to the surrounding universe.

Exercise 78 Stimulating Body Energy

Sit cross-legged on a mat or cushion, and bend your
right arm at the elbow so your right hand points to the
ceiling with the palm facing you. Make a fist. Place
your left thumb and middle finger exactly on the ends
or 'corners' of the elbow crease (pressure points 5 and
6 in Figure 5, page 119, Part 1). Support your elbow
from below with your left palm and grasp it tightly,

pressing strongly with both thumb and middle finger. You may feel a strong sensation at the joint. Lift
the elbow up a little so your right hand is at about the
same height as your head.

Now, facing forward, very slowly turn your torso
and arms to the right, continuing to press strongly
and steadily with your thumb and middle finger.
Take about thirty seconds for this movement. Relax
your neck (while still facing forward). Breathe very
lightly through both nose and mouth, and let the
breath bring more energy into your awareness.

When you have twisted to the right as far as you
can comfortably go, return to the front, again taking
about thirty seconds. Notice the quality of the
movement in this direction. Then very slowly release the pressure of your thumb and middle finger,
allowing your sensations to expand, and lower your
hands to your knees. Sit for a few minutes, continuing
to amplify the sensations in your body. You may feel
stimulated in the chest or heart center.

Now reverse the position of the arms and repeat
the movement to the left side, resting briefly afterward. Do the complete exercise, first one side, then
the other, three or nine times, resting a minute after
each repetition and for five to ten minutes at the end.

Exercise 79   Healing Energy

Sit cross-legged on a mat or cushion with your hands
on your knees. Slowly raise your left shoulder as high
as possible, and slowly lower your right shoulder as
much as possible. As you raise the left shoulder,
straighten your left arm, steadily pressing your hand
against your leg. Move your right elbow slightly out
to the side, so your right shoulder can lower more.

Face straight ahead, and let your head settle down between your shoulders.

Your left shoulder may come close to or even touch your left ear; do not, however, lean your head toward the shoulder. When you think you have stretched your shoulders apart as much as you can, relax for a few seconds, and then slowly stretch them apart a little more. Relax your lower belly, and allow it to curve in a natural way. Hold this position for three to five minutes or more, breathing easily through nose and mouth, with your throat relaxed. It is important to be very relaxed throughout this exercise.

Now gradually, in very slow motion, return your shoulders to their normal position. Take at least one minute to do this. Move as slowly as you can ever remember moving, and be aware of the interconnections among your feelings, senses, and awareness. You may feel a delicious warmth in your back and the back of your neck.

Now reverse the position of your shoulders, and repeat the exercise. Do the complete exercise (first one side, then the other) three times. At the end, sit quietly for five to ten minutes, expanding and deepening your feelings and sensations.

This exercise stimulates energy in the shoulders, neck, head, chest, and back.

Exercise 80   Nurturing Satisfaction

Sit cross-legged on a mat or cushion with your hands
on your knees. Bend your arms at the elbow, lifting
your hands until they are in front of your shoulders
with the palms facing forward. Imagine that a great
force is pushing against your hands, and slowly push
it away. Let strong tension build in your hands and
arms, but relax your belly and lower back, and

breathe easily and lightly through both nose and mouth. Keep pushing this force away until your arms are stretched out in front of you. Your hands and arms may shake with tension. Then without releasing the tension—as if the force is more powerful than you—slowly move your arms back in front of your chest, keeping your belly relaxed.

Now very slowly release the tension—take about one minute for this—feeling the sensations in your arms, chest, and body. Notice also the qualities of different stages of relaxation. Then slowly lower your hands to your knees and rest briefly, continuing to expand the feelings stimulated by producing and releasing tension in this way.

Do the exercise three times, resting briefly after each repetition. Then sit quietly in the sitting posture for five to ten minutes, continuing to expand the sensations in your body. You may feel an opening in your chest and upper back, and your breathing may be more open and free-flowing.

This exercise increases muscle strength in the arms, and relieves tension in the upper body. It can also be done standing.

Exercise 81   Stimulating the Present Body

Sit cross-legged on a mat or cushion with your elbows
held close against the sides of your body, your forearms vertical, and your palms facing forward. Imagine that you are pushing against the hands of someone stronger than you who is forcing your hands,
arms, and shoulders back. Very slowly move your
arms and shoulders back, letting the tension build.

Your fingers may tremble. Take at least one minute for this movement. Let your spine, neck, and chest be straight and very still; this will help to increase the energy. Relax your belly and lower back.

Now release the tension over a period of a minute, letting your arms move forward in the same plane. As you do this, look inward into your heart. Let your awareness be so sensitive that you can feel the subtle changes that occur in each instant. You may feel a deep emotional feeling like relief or being really satisfied. Perhaps there is a sensation of deep relaxation around your heart, and a melted quality to all of your muscles. You may feel sensations of heat or cold in the spine.

Slowly lower your hands to your knees and rest a minute, continuing to expand your sensations. Do the exercise three times, resting briefly after each repetition. At the end sit for five minutes or more, feeling the silent quality of this relaxation. As you continue to practice this exercise, hold your arms back for longer periods of time, and slow down the process of release even more.

Like the preceding exercise, this exercise builds muscle strength in the arms, and relieves tension in the **upper** body.

Exercise 82　Inner Massage

Sit cross-legged on a mat or cushion with your hands
on your knees. With your lower body as relaxed as
possible, move your shoulder blades back toward
each other, squeezing the big muscles along the sides
of the spine. In this position, slowly raise your
shoulders as high as you can, settling your neck down
between them in such a way that you are almost

pushing your neck down, and your chin comes close to your chest. Feel the backbone lifting all the way down to your sacrum. With your shoulder blades in the same position, slowly lower your shoulders, massaging down the spinal muscles. Now slowly, expanding your feelings, release the tension.

Do the exercise again, this time coordinating your breathing with the movement. Inhale as you raise your shoulders; then briefly hold the breath in your chest, with your stomach a little held in. Slowly lower your shoulders, and begin to exhale when your shoulders are at a nearly normal level. Exhale so slowly and smoothly that the exhalation becomes almost silent. Continue the exercise, three or nine times, then sit quietly for five to ten minutes.

☆ Now try this variation. Move your shoulder blades back toward each other, and slowly raise your shoulders as high as possible, simultaneously pushing your neck down into your body with your chin close to your chest. Then very slowly relax the tension, lifting your head as if someone were pulling you up from the top of your head, and at the same time letting your shoulders move down. Concentrate on the upward movement of your head and feel the upward stretch along the whole length of your backbone. You may feel sensations of lightness and energy throughout a central column in your body, and a healing feeling in the center of the bones, a special kind of energy and warmth.

Do this version of the spinal massage very slowly three times, and then sit for five to ten minutes, exercising your sensations and feelings.

Exercise 83   Stimulating Vital Energy

Sit cross-legged on a mat or cushion with your hands resting on your knees. Visualize the spine as a slightly arching bow, without actually bending forward. Flatten your belly against your spine, and lightly push out the spine of the middle back, as if pushing the vertebrae apart. The movement in your spine can be quite subtle. As you do this, relax your hands, and lower your head a little, while keeping your chest up. Hold this position for three to five minutes, breathing gently and evenly through both nose and mouth, and concentrating lightly on lengthening the spine of your middle back.

After three to five minutes, slowly straighten your spine, feeling warm, calm, healing energy flow through the whole length of your spine, relaxing you and bringing a sensitive, joyful sensation. Sit quietly for a minute, continuing to expand the sensations in your body.

Do the exercise three or nine times, sitting briefly after each repetition. At the end, sit for five to ten minutes, expanding the sensations flowing through your spine to the rest of your body, and beyond it to the surrounding environment.

Exercise 84   Stimulating the Essence of Vitality

Sit cross-legged on a mat or cushion with your hands on your knees, and your back straight. Breathe easily through both nose and mouth. Slowly begin to compress your spine, letting each vertebra sink down close to the next, all the way down your spine, until you feel the root of your body sink into the ground. Take at least one minute to do this, continuing to breathe slowly and evenly through both nose and mouth. Go deeply into the sensations of this movement.

Now, beginning at the base of your spine, begin to lift the vertebrae away from each other, feeling space open within as well as between the bones. Do this very slowly, letting the spaces expand and flow together until they have no boundaries. Let the subtle energy of the breath enter and become part of this vast, expanding space.

When you lift the spine of your neck, imagine that the top of your head is being drawn toward the sky. Feel the sensation of space expanding as you stretch slightly upwards. Taste the special quality of this relaxation. Sit for three to five minutes, expanding your sensations.

Do the exercise three times, sitting for a few minutes after each repetition and for five to ten minutes at the end.

Exercise 85 Being and Energy

Sit on the floor or ground with your palms on the floor near your hips and your right leg stretched out in front of you. Flex your right ankle so the toes point toward your head, and place your left foot against the inside of your right knee, with your left knee on the floor, if possible.

Now push your left foot against your right knee,

and push your right knee against your left foot until your legs are almost shaking. You may be able to push harder with the left leg than with the right. Hold the tension for thirty seconds to one minute, with your belly relaxed, breathing easily through both nose and mouth. Then very slowly release the tension and rest in this position, expanding the sensations in your body.

Now reverse the position of the legs and repeat the exercise. Do the complete movement, first one side, then the other, three times. When you finish, sit in the sitting posture for five to ten minutes, continuing to expand your feelings and sensations.

This exercise activates pressure points on the knee and foot. (See Figures 7 and 8, pp. 129 and 135 respectively, Part 1.) Especially as you release the pressure, unify breath, awareness, and sensation, allowing the many subtle flavors of feeling to merge and expand.

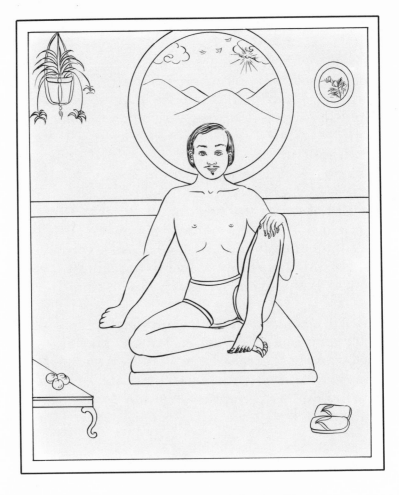

Exercise 86 Stimulating Healthy Feeling

Sit barefoot on the floor or ground with your legs loosely crossed, the right leg outside the left. Make a fist with your left hand, and turn the fist so the inner side of it—the index finger and the thumb—points toward the floor. Place the fist in this position on the floor quite close behind you, so you are supported by your left arm. Lift the right knee and place the right foot across the left foot, arch to arch, with the toes and ball of the right foot on the floor. Place your right hand on your right knee.

Now slowly rock forward and backward: push your right knee down toward the floor, lift your left hip, stand on your right toes, and at the same time stretch your upper body back a little, being careful not to stretch your toes too much. Then without holding, rock back onto your pelvis. Notice that as you do this movement, the arches of both feet are massaged.

If you find the exercise difficult to do with the left hand in a fist, try it with the palm flat on the floor. Also try placing the left hand different distances from your body; the stretch will be stronger when the hand is nearer the body.

Stretch the toes in this way three or nine times on the right side, then reverse the position of your arms and legs, and repeat the movement three or nine times on the left side. Then sit in the sitting posture for five to ten minutes, expanding the sensations produced by releasing tension and stimulating pressure points in this way.

Exercise 87   Transmuting Negative Energies

Sit cross-legged on a mat or cushion with your hands
on your knees, and close your eyes in a relaxed way.
Softly and gently feel warmth and a kind of sweet-
ness in a place where you feel tight and uncomfortable. Subtle, accepting feelings will come. At first
focus your concentration there; then apply less and
less concentration, while still experiencing the subtle

qualities of feeling. Listen to the feelings with your internal senses. Attend to how feeling enters your heart, throat, back, the back of your neck, your lower stomach, your hands, your skin—wherever you have a sensation of holding or tightness. Let every cell in your body be relaxed; hold nothing. Let tension in your forehead go, and relax the areas around your eyes and ears.

Let subtle energies float and find new pathways in your body. Let the looseness of your concentration become a feeling quality, as if you were very lightly swimming, swaying. In a very light way, keep increasing the sensation of movement. Expand the feeling, going deeper and deeper, beyond what seem to be the limits of the feeling. Let the feeling become larger until finally there is nothing but the feeling, and your mind and senses become one. Thoughts, concepts, and feelings merge together, mind and senses flow together, embracing each other, merging totally.

At first concentrate like this for twenty minutes at a time, once or twice a day for a week. Then if you want to explore further, continue your internal listening and expansion of these subtle feelings for an hour a day for a month.

Exercise 88 Stimulating Inner Body Energies

Stand well balanced with your back and neck straight, and your feet a comfortable distance apart. Slowly stretch out your right arm to the side at shoulder height, with the palm down. With your left hand, grasp the muscle which connects the right shoulder and arm, putting your fingers in the armpit and pressing with your thumb a pressure point on the right extremity of the chest. (This is point 7 in Figure 5, p. 119, Part 1.)

Hold the muscle firmly and push it upward and into your chest. Keeping your arm straight and your palm down, very slowly rotate your right arm in the largest circle possible. Breathe gently through both nose and mouth, and look straight ahead, with your back straight and your head still. Very slowly, taking about one minute for each circle, draw three or nine circles; then find a place where it feels natural to change direction and draw three or nine circles the other way.

When you finish, stand without moving for a few minutes, with your eyes closed, and feel the flow of energies in your body. Be aware of sensations in your chest, especially the heart and lung areas.

Now repeat the slow circles with your left arm, three or nine times in each direction. Try making some of the circles different sizes to produce different tones of feeling. Then sit for five to ten minutes, expanding the sensations quickened by this exercise.

☆ Here is another version of the above exercise. Raise your right arm overhead and make a fist. With the left hand, grasp the muscle on the right side of the chest in the manner described above. Hold the muscle firmly and push it upward and into your chest. Keeping your arm straight, very slowly rotate your right arm forward, drawing the largest circle possible to the side of your body. Your arm will move close to your right leg and near your right ear during the slow rotation. Breathe easily and relax your belly and spine; only your arms are slightly tensed. Make three or nine slow circles in this direction, then three or nine slow circles in the opposite direction. Pay close attention to feelings in your shoulders, back, neck, and chest.

When you have completed the circles with your right arm, stand quietly for a few minutes to feel the sensations in your body. Then very slowly repeat the movement with your left arm. Make sure that the circles are at the side of your body, and remember to breathe gently and evenly through both nose and mouth. At the conclusion of the exercise, sit in the sitting posture for five to ten minutes, feeling the movement of energies within you.

Like Exercise 94 and other exercises and massages, this exercise combines movement with pressure on a certain point. You might want to try pressing the point before beginning the movement, going deeply into the feelings that are produced. Then slowly develop the movement, using it to deepen, distribute and expand your sensations. Experiment with different degrees of pressure as the arm rotates, and follow the subtle changes in feeling-tone during each part of the movement. Be sure to release the pressure very slowly and gradually.

Exercise 89 Transforming Energy

Stand well balanced with your feet a comfortable
distance apart, your back straight, and your arms at
your sides. Clench your fists strongly, hold your
breath back in the chest, and tighten your chest until
you feel something similar in quality to anger. Then
breathing very lightly—without losing the feeling of
holding back in the chest—bring your elbows and fists

to chest height, strongly press your fists together knuckle to knuckle, and place them in the center of your chest.

Make your body and fists very strong and tense. Slowly inhale deeply so your breath rolls down into your belly and draws energy from the base of the spine up into your chest. Hold this energy back internally with the breath and with your chest, as if protecting yourself. Intensify the feeling of blocking and holding back as much as you can, so your energy becomes concentrated.

Now with your body still, suddenly, in an instant, thrust your arms straight out, palms forward, releasing all the gathered energy in an explosion, while fully and sharply exhaling, shouting HA from your chest. It is very important for this movement of the arms to be straight forward, and for the hands to be bent up at the wrists. Every aspect of the tension—physical, mental and emotional—is released simultaneously. Stay for a moment with outstretched arms, fingers wide. In the pause after the explosion, what is the feeling?

Now slowly lower your arms to your sides, and stand quietly for a few minutes. Do the exercise three times, standing briefly after each repetition. Then sit in the sitting posture for five to ten minutes, expanding the sensations stimulated by producing and releasing tension in this way. It is also possible to do this exercise nine times, repeating this pattern of exercise and sitting three times.

Through this exercise, mental agitation and emotional discomfort can be transformed. As soon as energy is disconnected from a particular pattern, a new way of being can form. Try this exercise when you feel tired, depressed, negative, or blocked. The exercise can also be done sitting.

Once you are familiar with this exercise, try the following variations:

☆   Do the exercise as described above. After releasing the tension and shouting HA, stay for a moment with outstretched arms, expanding the feeling at the pause. As you slowly lower your arms, gather that feeling and bring it into your body. Stand quietly for a few minutes; then repeat the exercise twice more. Sit afterward for five to ten minutes, continuing to exercise your sensations: expanding them, then drawing them back into your body.

☆   This variation develops a subtle inner transformation. Do the exercise as described in the first version. After releasing the tension and shouting HA, stay in the pause for a moment. As you slowly let your arms down, gently hold the breath up in your chest until it dissolves into a subtle inner feeling or 'breath' in the chest. When it becomes too hard to hold the breath up, let it gradually ease down to a point of balance lower in your body. When it becomes too difficult to hold the breath at this point, let it move down to a lower point of balance. Continue this process, gradually lowering the breath in your body until the sensation can hardly be felt. Then repeat the exercise.

Do the exercise three times. Then sit quietly for ten or fifteen minutes, allowing this subtle inner feeling of breath to expand.

Exercise 90 Living Breath

Stand well balanced with your feet a comfortable distance apart, your back straight, and your arms relaxed at your sides. Interlace your fingers and place them at the back of your neck, with the elbows wide apart and your chest high. Breathe gently through both nose and mouth.

Bend your knees a little and arch your back and

neck slightly backwards. Make sure your chest is high and your body relaxed and balanced.

Then take two, three, or four quick, gasp-like intakes of breath from the belly, and exhale as slowly as possible, attending particularly to the sensations in your belly area. Let the breath massage you internally. Picture the breath passing from the bloodstream into all of your internal organs, suffusing each cell, even each molecule, with vital, relaxing sensation. See if you can sense the subtle inner quality of this massage of the breath.

Do the exercise three or nine times; then sit for five to ten minutes, continuing to expand the sensations of this internal massage.

This exercise relieves tension in the belly area, and lightens negative patterns such as resistance.

Exercise 91   Activating Healing Energy

Stand well balanced with your feet a few inches apart, your back straight, and your arms relaxed at your sides. Stretch your arms out to your sides at shoulder height, with the palms down. Move your head back slightly so you look at where the wall meets the ceiling. Relax your neck, open your mouth, and flare your nostrils. Breathe easily through both nose and mouth.

Now relax your belly and chest as fully as you can; bring your attention to the base of your spine, and tighten your buttocks. Hold for three to five minutes, continuing to concentrate on the base of your spine. Be sure to keep your belly and chest very relaxed. If mild shaking or trembling develops, go into it and release tension. Breathe very softly and evenly.

When you feel something at the base of the spine, perhaps heat or a tingling sensation, expand that feeling as much as you can to your back, arms, head, and your whole body. However, if you feel strong heat rising up your spine, do not continue the exercise; instead, gently lower your arms, straighten your head, and sit in the sitting posture for five to ten minutes, expanding the sensations in your body.

After holding the position for three to five minutes, slowly lower your arms to your sides, straighten your head, and stand relaxed for several minutes, expanding the sensations in your body. Do the exercise three times, standing relaxed after each repetition. Then sit in the sitting posture for five to ten minutes, continuing to expand the feelings activated by the exercise.

A variation of this exercise is done with the knees bent. Experiment to see how feeling is affected by different degrees of bending in the knees.

Exercise 92 Channeling Body Energy into the Senses

This exercise is a little strenuous; if you are an older person unused to regular exercise, it is best not to do this one.

Lie on your back with your arms stretched out to your sides at shoulder height, with the palms up. Separate your legs the width of your pelvis, and flex your ankles so that the toes of both feet point toward your head. Sliding your heel along the floor until it lifts naturally, bend your left knee and bring your thigh close to your torso, while keeping your right leg straight. Draw your thigh strongly toward your body. Breathing softly through both nose and mouth, hold the tension in your legs and feet for fifteen to thirty seconds, keeping your arms and shoulders relaxed. Then very slowly release the tension, straighten your leg, and relax your feet, expanding the sensations stimulated by producing and releasing tension in this way. Rest briefly on your back.

Now flex your ankles, bend your right knee, bring the thigh close to your torso, and repeat the exercise. Do the complete exercise, first on one side, then the other, three times, resting for a few minutes after each repetition. When you finish, rest on your back for five to ten minutes, keeping your arms out-stretched at shoulder height, palms up, and continue to amplify and extend the sensations in your body.

A variation of this exercise is done with both thighs pressed to the body at once; this version may produce more intense feelings.

Stage Three

These exercises are generally more advanced than those in Stages One and Two. Some are quite strenuous physically; in others a certain quality of concentration is needed to develop the feeling-tones that are stimulated. You should therefore wait until you have deepened your experience of Kum Nye over a period of several months before you try these exercises.

When you feel ready, add one or two of these exercises to your practice. Do not push yourself, however, and wait until you have had even more experience before trying the last ten exercises.

If you have not already done so, you might now want to practice some of the exercises at different tempos. Begin with an exercise you know well, and try it in different ways. First do the exercise slowly, and then, without losing touch with the feeling-tones, build up a little speed. Then develop the different feeling-tones generated at the different tempos.

You will also find that all of the exercises done tensely can be done in a relaxed way, and those done 'loosely' can also be done tensely. As your awareness of subtle inner feelings grows, you will discover how to use both tempo and tension to strengthen and expand the feeling-tones of each exercise.

Let your practice of Kum Nye be an open-ended journey into your inner senses and feelings. As your body and mind become more integrated, your experience of greater balance will itself become your guide.

Exercise 93   Refreshing the Senses

Sit cross-legged on a mat or cushion with your hands
on your knees and your back straight. Slowly lift your
arms away from your sides to shoulder height, with
the palms facing behind you, and then lower them
until they are at about a forty-five degree angle from
your body. Lift your shoulders as high as possible,
and tuck your chin in a little.

In this position, imagine that a person stronger than you is pushing against your hands and arms, forcing them backward. Maintain strong tension in your hands and arms, relax your belly and lower back, and very slowly move your hands and arms back and up a little. It is not necessary to go very far back or up. With your body still, your chest open, and your spine balanced, hold this position for one minute or ten to fifteen outbreaths. Breathe gently and evenly through both nose and mouth.

Release the tension as slowly as you can, sensing the feelings generated by holding in this way. Then bring your hands to your knees and rest a minute, letting the ripples of sensation move· through and beyond your body. Do the exercise three times, resting briefly after each repetition. At the end, sit for five to ten minutes, continuing to expand the feelings that have arisen during the exercise.

This exercise releases both physical and psychological tension, and stimulates the flow of sensation throughout the body.

Exercise 94   Nurturing Body Energy

Sit cross-legged on a mat or cushion, and run your
fingers along your collarbone until you feel it meet
the bone of your shoulder. Make light fists with your
fingers and press your thumbs gently into the de-
pressions on the lower side of the collarbone. With
your mouth open slightly, breathing evenly through
both nose and mouth, slowly jut out your jaw. As

you do so, gradually increase the pressure of your thumbs until the pressure is quite strong. Hold for one to three minutes, going deeply into your sensations. Notice the quality of your breath, for it will reveal your emotional state. Allow whatever emotions or sensations you feel to come to the surface.

Then very slowly release the tension in your thumbs, neck, and jaw, allowing your sensations to fill the field of experience. Sit quietly for several minutes with your hands on your knees, expanding your feelings throughout your body.

Now repeat the exercise. If you find primitive sounds arising within you, perhaps expressions of rage or pain, express them. You may want to make sounds during the entire period of holding.

Again, very slowly release the tension, and sit quietly for several minutes. What are the qualities of your breathing? What is your state of mind?

Do the exercise three or nine times, resting for a few minutes after each repetition and for five to ten minutes at the end.

Exercise 95   Stimulating Inner Energy

This exercise is especially effective when done after massaging the back of the neck.

Sit cross-legged on a mat or cushion, press your palms together, and turn your hands so your finger-tips touch the center of your chest. As you inhale, push inside and a little up (do this more with the breath than with your hands), and stretch your neck upward a little, with your chin in. Now hold your breath, press your chin strongly in, and inwardly make a push to the back of your neck. You may feel sensations of warmth there. Continue to hold your breath for as long as you can, and expand your sensations, letting them flow down your spine and spread throughout your body.

Now slowly exhale and release the tension, letting your subtle inner feelings radiate throughout your whole body and spread to the surrounding environment. Let the boundaries between inner and outer spaces melt. Sit quietly for several minutes, sensing the feelings within and around you.

Do the exercise three or nine times, sitting after each repetition, and at the end.

Certain positions produce certain energies. In this exercise, a certain positive energy builds up until it nurtures the whole body.

Exercise 96   Wholeness of Joy

Do this exercise very gently if you are pregnant, if
you have had any sort of back or neck injury, or if
you have had an operation within three or four months.

Sit cross-legged on a mat or cushion or on a low
stool with your back straight. Grasp your knees
strongly for support and lift your chest toward the
ceiling. Be sure to hold your knees firmly with your

hands, so there is a feeling of strength in your arms, knees, and hands. As your back arches, open your mouth and let your chin move toward the ceiling. Do not let your head go all the way back, for too extreme a curve in the neck will interrupt the flow of sensation. Breathe softly and evenly through both nose and mouth. Relax your belly; this will make it possible to stretch the spine backward a little more, but be careful not to strain. Hold for one to three minutes, sensing the feelings in your chest and spine.

When you feel heat warming the back of your neck, very slowly and gradually move forward, straightening your spine. As you release the tension, be aware of sensations of heat and energy that may extend beyond the ordinary limits of your body. You may feel a deep joy. Do the exercise three or nine times, resting in the sitting posture for a few minutes after each repetition and for five to ten minutes at the end.

Exercise 97   Touching Time

Sit on a mat or cushion, place the soles of your feet
together, and draw them as close to your body as
possible. Put your hands on your kneecaps, lift your
elbows a little, and press down. Both elbows should
be at the same height, and your shoulders level. In
this position, stretch your upper back up a little, and
settle your neck down between your shoulders. Then

very slowly bend forward from the waist as low as you can, relaxing the thigh socket as much as possible. Stay down for one to three minutes, breathing gently through both nose and mouth. Then very slowly straighten your spine, feeling the sensations in your body. If staying down is too difficult, then slowly straighten your spine without holding. Rest briefly, expanding the sensations quickened by the exercise.

Do the exercise three or nine times, sitting quietly for a few minutes after each repetition and for five to ten minutes at the end, continuing to expand the sensations within and around your body.

This exercise stretches the thigh and back muscles, releasing energies held in the thigh socket, the sacrum, and the spine.

Exercise 98   Inner Immortality of Energy

Kneel on your left knee and place your right foot flat on the floor just in front of the left knee, so the heel and knee touch. Lift your left foot a little, and stand on your left toes; then sit all the way back so your left buttock rests on your left ankle. (Be alert and sensitive to the left toes during the exercise, so you do not put too much weight on them. If they become painful, straighten the foot so the toes point behind you and do the exercise that way.) Place your hands on the floor to the left of your body, widely separated, with the fingers of the right hand pointing in the same direction as the right foot, and the fingers of the left hand pointing in the opposite direction. Keeping both arms straight, twist your head and torso to the right so your left shoulder moves down, and your right shoulder moves up a little. Look up toward the ceiling, with your chin near your right shoulder. Breathe evenly through both nose and mouth, and feel the sensations produced by this twist in your spine. Hold for thirty seconds to one minute.

To change your position so you can do the twist to the left, slowly straighten your neck and let your head hang down in a relaxed way; then slide your hands along the floor toward each other until they are about a foot apart, with the fingers pointing left (i.e. left in relation to your body). Standing on your left toes, lift your left knee and swing it a little to the left, then lift your right heel so you stand also on your right toes, and swivel both feet until they point in the same direction as your hands. Lower your head and lift your pelvis toward the ceiling until your legs are almost straight. Swivel your toes to the left, kneel on your right knee, place your left heel in front of your right knee, and separate your hands, pointing the fingers of the left hand in the same direction as the left foot and the fingers of the right hand in the opposite direction. In this position, keeping your arms straight, and breathing gently through both nose and mouth, do the spinal twist to the left.

Do the complete exercise, twisting first to one side, then to the other, three times. Then sit in the sitting posture for five to ten minutes, expanding the sensations stimulated by this movement.

Exercises 99 through 102 stimulate joyful feelings, activate sexual energies and distribute them throughout the body, relieve negative patterns such as resistance, and vitalize inner energies. In all of these exercises, the muscles of the backs of the legs are stretched. In most people, these muscles are quite contracted, so be sensitive and alert when doing an exercise not to stretch too much. The exercises will be effective with even a slight stretch. If you are an older person unused to regular exercise, it may be best not to attempt these exercises. In any case, do them gently, slowly easing into the stretch, and developing a quality of lightness.

Explore each exercise fully before trying another. Do not be in a rush. Each exercise stimulates slightly different feeling-tones, and it is possible to become very sensitive to the subtle flavors of each. You do not need to do the exercises in the sequence presented here.

You may feel more, and be less likely to stretch too much, if you massage the backs of your legs before doing an exercise. For the massage, lie on your back, bend your knees one at a time, and place your feet flat on the floor. Bring your right knee close to your chest, then straighten the leg toward the ceiling, supporting the back of the thigh with interlaced hands. Move the leg back and forth slowly and lightly a few times.

Then gently point first the toe and then the heel to the ceiling three or four times.

Now lock your leg straight with the foot parallel to the ceiling, and grasp the back of the thigh with both hands so your fingers meet in the middle. Massage the back of the thigh firmly in horizontal strokes, working from the center out to the sides. Work up the back of the leg toward the foot, lifting your head if necessary to help you reach the lower leg. Breathe gently through both nose and mouth as you stroke, letting the breath merge with both motion and sensation.

When you finish, slowly bend the right knee and lower the right foot to the floor. Rest for a few minutes, expanding the sensations generated by the massage. Then repeat the massage for the left leg.

Exercise 99 Touching Positive Feeling

With your feet a few inches apart, squat on the toes and balls of your feet, and with your arms outside of your legs, place your palms flat on the floor in front of you, the fingers pointing forward. Look up toward the ceiling, breathing gently through nose and mouth.

Keeping your palms flat on the floor, slowly lower your head, lift your pelvis toward the ceiling as far as you can without straining, and lower your heels to the floor. Feel the stretch in the backs of your legs, being sure not to stretch too much. Hold for thirty seconds to one minute, relaxing your feet and belly, letting your head hang loosely from your neck, and breathing as evenly as possible through both nose and mouth. If your legs tremble or shake, go into the shaking and release tensions.

Now very slowly lower your pelvis, lift your head and heels, squat briefly on the toes and balls of your feet, and then sit in the sitting posture for one to two minutes, expanding the sensations stimulated by the leg stretch. You may feel warmth moving up your legs into your pelvis. Expand these sensations to your spine, your upper body, your arms and head. Feel them more. Let them permeate every cell in your whole body.

Do the exercise three times, sitting after each repetition and for five to ten minutes at the end, expanding and distributing the feelings awakened by the exercise.

Exercise 100   Wholesome Energy

With your feet a few inches apart, squat on the toes and balls of your feet. Make fists, and with your arms outside your legs, place the first and second knuckles of the fists flat on the floor. Then place the thumbs flat on the floor, pointing toward each other.

Keeping your fists and thumbs on the floor, slowly lower your head, lift your pelvis toward the ceiling as

high as you can without straining, and lower your
heels to the floor. Remember to ease into the stretch
in a light and gentle way. (If you find it too difficult to
straighten your legs, do not be concerned. When you
stay with your sensations, and continue to relax
subtle tensions, the exercise will be effective.) When
your pelvis is as high as it can comfortably be, look
up, and hold this position for thirty seconds to one
minute, breathing gently through both nose and
mouth. Concentrate lightly on your feelings.

After thirty seconds to one minute, slowly lower
your head, lower your pelvis, lift your heels, squat
briefly on the toes and balls of your feet, and then sit
quietly in the sitting posture for one to two minutes,
expanding the feelings quickened by the leg stretch.

Do the exercise three times, sitting after each repetition and for five to ten minutes at the end, expanding the sensations within and around your body.

Exercise 101   Touching Present Energy

With your feet apart about the width of your pelvis,
squat on the toes and balls of your feet and widely
separate your knees. Turn your arms so the inner arm
faces forward and the fingers point behind you, and
with your arms inside your legs, place your hands flat
on the floor a little further apart than your feet. Look
straight ahead, with your chest as high as possible.

Keeping your hands flat on the floor, slowly lower your head, lift your pelvis as high as you can without straining and lower your heels to the floor. Relax your neck and let your head hang. Feel the stretch in the backs of your legs and in your arms, but be sure not to stretch too much. Stay in this position for thirty seconds to one minute, breathing evenly through both nose and mouth, and relaxing your feet and belly. If your legs shake, go into the shaking and release as much tension as you can.

Slowly lower your pelvis, lift your heels, lift your head, squat briefly on the toes and balls of your feet with your chest high, and then sit in the sitting posture for one to two minutes, expanding the sensations quickened by the stretch.

Do the exercise three times, sitting for a few minutes after each repetition and for five to ten minutes at the end, continuing to amplify the feelings within and around your body.

Exercise 102   Texture of Joy

Get down on your hands and knees, with a pillow under just the knees. Point your fingers forward. Lift your feet a little and stand on your toes, so your weight is balanced on your toes, knees, and hands. Keeping your palms flat on the floor and your arms straight, slowly lower your head, shift your weight forward a little, and lift your knees until your legs are straight. Then lower your heels to the ground. Hold this stretch for thirty seconds to one minute, breathing gently through both nose and mouth, and feeling the sensations in the backs of your legs. Let your head hang loosely from your neck. If you cannot bring your heels all the way to the ground, lower them as far as you can without straining the muscles of the backs of your legs, and hold the stretch in this position. Bringing your hands closer to your body will also decrease the stretch. In time you may find that you can bring your heels all the way to the floor.

After thirty seconds to a minute, very slowly bend your knees and lower them to the pillow, sensing the feelings stimulated in your body as you release the stretch. Rest briefly on your hands and knees with your feet relaxed, soles up, continuing to expand the sensations quickened by the movement.

Do the exercise three times, resting after each repetition. At the end, sit in the sitting posture for five to ten minutes, continuing to expand the sensations produced by the exercise.

☆ The following version of this exercise is a little more strenuous. To take the position illustrated in the drawing, kneel on a mat and locate a spot about one foot in front of your left knee. Lift your left leg and place your left foot on that spot. Lift your right foot a little and stand on the toes. Then place your palms flat on the floor in front of you, a shoulder width apart, with your fingers pointing forward.

Now keeping your palms flat on the floor, slowly lower your head, lift your right knee and lower your right heel to the floor, straightening *both* legs as much as possible. Hold the stretch for thirty seconds to one minute. Be sure to keep your palms flat on the floor. Then slowly bend your right knee and lower it to the mat, feeling the sensations released in your body. Rest briefly on hands and knees, with your feet relaxed, soles up.

Now reverse the position of your legs and repeat the exercise. Do the complete movement, first on one side, then on the other, three times, resting briefly after each stretch. At the end, sit in the sitting posture for five to ten minutes, allowing the feelings stimulated by this exercise to be distributed throughout your body, and beyond it to the surrounding environment.

Exercise 103   Vitality

Kneel on a mat or soft pillow with your thighs vertical. Lift your feet a little and stand on your toes, being
careful not to put too much pressure on them. (If the
exercise is difficult for you with your toes in this
position, straighten your feet so the toes point behind
you, and do the exercise that way.) Interlace your
fingers and place them at the back of your neck, with
the elbows wide apart.

In this position, breathing gently through both nose and mouth, very slowly arch backward without straining, and hold for fifteen to thirty seconds. Feel the sensations in the small of your back, and relax your throat, chest, and belly as much as possible.

Then very slowly—it is important to move very slowly throughout this exercise—straighten your spine and sit back on your heels. Then lifting first one knee and then the other, squat on the toes and balls of your feet with your heels together. Spread your knees wide apart and slowly bend forward as far as possible, keeping the elbows wide apart. Let your head hang loosely from your neck.

Hold for fifteen to thirty seconds, breathing easily through both nose and mouth, feeling the sensations in your spine. Then very slowly straighten back up, bring your knees closer together, and move from squatting to kneeling (kneel first on one knee and then on the other), slowly raising your pelvis until your thighs are vertical. Then slowly arch backward, beginning the movement again. Except for the two points of holding, this exercise is done as a continuous movement.

Do the exercise *very slowly* three times, breathing easily through both nose and mouth, and concentrating lightly on the sensations in your spine. To complete the exercise, sit in the sitting posture for five to ten minutes, expanding the sensations within and around your body.

A variation of this exercise is done with the hands clasped at the back of the head. Notice the different sensations produced by the different stretch.

This exercise revitalizes the whole body, increases stability, and improves coordination.

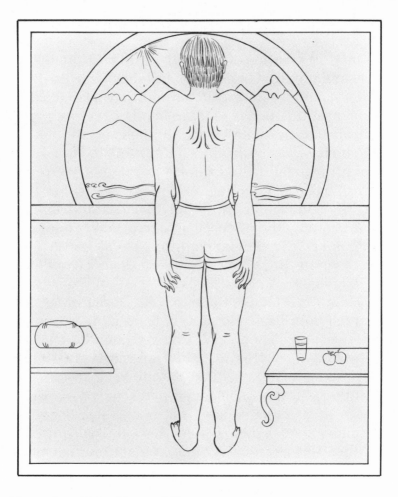

Exercise 104   Sacred Energy

Stand well balanced with your feet a comfortable distance apart, your back straight, and your arms relaxed at your sides. Move your shoulders back as far as you can, squeezing your shoulder blades together. When you think you have moved your shoulders back as far as possible, move them back more. Now move them back a little more, until you can almost feel thick wrinkles in the skin of your back between the shoulder blades. Keeping your shoulders back, lift them a little, and grasp your thighs with your hands. Your back, arms, and shoulders are very tense. Relax your chin and settle your neck down between your shoulders. Hold this position for one to three minutes, breathing gently through both nose and mouth, with the front of your body as relaxed as possible. Relax your thighs.

Now very slowly release the tension—take about one minute for this—and stand with your arms relaxed at your sides for one to two minutes, letting subtle qualities of feeling spread throughout your body. Do the exercise three times, standing in a relaxed way after each repetition. To complete the exercise, sit in the sitting posture for five to ten minutes, allowing the feelings quickened by this movement to expand.

This exercise stimulates heat which moves to the inner core of the body and balances the energies of the front and back of the body.

Exercise 105   Heart Gold Thread

Stand well balanced with your feet about six inches
apart, your back straight, and your arms relaxed at
your sides. Slowly lift your arms away from your
sides to a little above shoulder height, with the palms
down. Bend the elbows very slightly. Close your eyes,
and bring your awareness and concentration to
your heart center. Sense the heart pumping blood

throughout your body; then expand and deepen your awareness, sending the energy of the heart center outward through your arms. Breathe very lightly and evenly, through both nose and mouth. Standing very still, gently hold this position for ten minutes. After two or three minutes, slightly loosen the muscles on the top of your shoulder joint; this may make the position easier to hold.

After ten minutes, lower your arms very slowly and gently, taking about one minute to lower them all the way down to your sides. Stand silently with your arms at your sides for a few minutes, expanding the sensations generated by this posture. Then lie down on your back for ten minutes, continuing to amplify these sensations until they spread even beyond your body.

This exercise balances the heart center, increases mental and physical energy, improves circulation (and the complexion), and builds strength and concentration. The exercise can also be an instrument for identifying and transforming psychological and physical blockages. As you do it, notice weak or tense areas of your body; notice also the times at which you lose strength and concentration and want to give up. If you feel fear. or pain, bring this feeling into your heart center, and touch it with concentration and awareness.

A memory of an emotion may come into your mind, perhaps sorrow, hurt, or pain. Expand the feeling as much as you can, letting your senses and your mind become one. Stay with the feeling until you penetrate it and release it into pure experience. A flash of energy—the energy of that memory—then enters the present, and the pattern of the emotion melts, and no longer exists. Then you are beyond the pain, surrounded by an expressive quality which means you are no longer holding—a quality of 'here I am' which can be observed and felt in every cell of your body.

You feel a sense of union, a willingness to let feelings arise and expand, and you are able to embrace experience directly, without hesitation. With more experience, it is possible to face pain, fear, and tension directly, letting them go as they occur in daily life.

As you become familiar with this exercise, try holding the position for longer periods of time, up to twenty-five minutes. Rest afterwards for as long as you held the position, standing and then lying down, or if you wish, simply lying down.

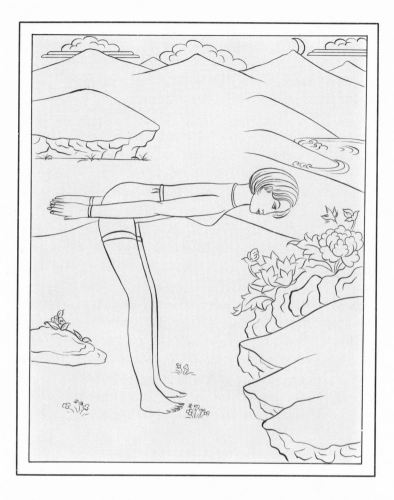

Exercise 106   Trinity of Practice: Breath, Energy, and Awareness

Stand well balanced with your feet a few inches apart, your back straight, and your arms relaxed at your sides. Extend your arms in front of you, palms together, with the fingers pointing straight ahead. In one continuous movement, stretch your arms forward and push your pelvis backward, lowering your head between your arms, until your torso, head, and arms are parallel to the ground. Keep your back straight throughout this movement.

In this position, stretch forward with the arms and at the same time, stretch the pelvis backward. The knees are straight. Do not hold your breath; breathe as evenly as you can through both nose and mouth. Interlace the fingers and stretch more, in both directions; your body will lower a little. Stretch even more, until you feel you have touched a place of energy. You may begin to shake. Hold for fifteen to thirty seconds.

Now, without releasing the tension, very slowly move your hands apart, and keeping your arms at the same level, move them in an arc, palms down, until they are straight in back of you and close to your body. In this position, stretch your neck forward and your pelvis backward until you feel the energy. Hold as long as you can, breathing evenly through both nose and mouth.

Then very slowly release the tension and stand up, carrying your weight in the legs. Stand silently for three to five minutes and then repeat the exercise twice, resting after each repetition. Then sit in the sitting posture for fifteen minutes, broadening your sensations until they spread out to the universe, and you are aware of nothing else. You may feel openings along the spine and in your chest, hands, neck, and head.

This exercise stimulates and revitalizes inner energies, and builds strength and concentration.

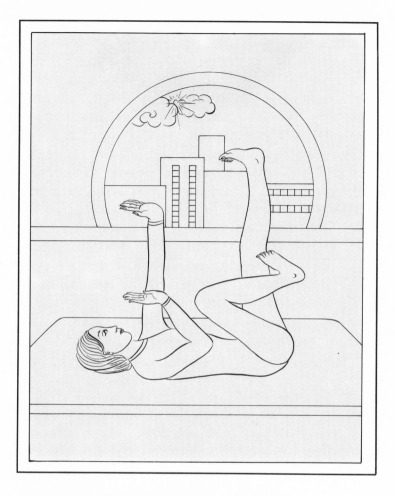

Exercise 107   Expanding Inner Energy

Lie down on your back with your legs a comfortable
distance apart and your arms at your sides. Bend your
knees, one at a time, and bring them close to your
chest. Flex your ankles so the toes point toward your
head. (They will stay this way throughout the exercise.) Slide your arms along the floor until they are
stretched out at shoulder height, with the palms

up. In this position, draw your thighs strongly toward your torso. When you do this, you will feel the muscle in the top of the thigh which controls this movement. Relax your shoulders, neck, and arms, and breathe gently through both nose and mouth.

Now while still keeping your left thigh as close to your body as you can, slowly extend your right leg (with the ankle flexed) toward the ceiling. Feel the contraction in the left thigh, and the extension in the right. Then slowly bend the right knee and bring the right thigh as close to your body as you can, and at the same time, extend the left leg toward the ceiling. Keep your upper body and your belly as relaxed as possible throughout the movement. Let breath and awareness expand your sensations and become one with the movement.

Do the complete movement (including both sides of the body) three continuous times. Then slowly lower the left leg, release the tension, and one at a time, bring your feet back to the floor and straighten your legs. Rest on your back for five to ten minutes, expanding the sensations stimulated by this movement.

☆ When you become familiar with the above exercise, try this variation: lie on your back with your legs a comfortable distance apart, and your arms close to your body, bent at the elbows so your palms face the ceiling. Bend your knees one at a time and bring them close to your chest. Flex your ankles so the toes point toward your head. Imagine that a strong force is pushing against your hands, making tension in your arms as well as in your legs.

Maintaining the tension in your left arm and leg, slowly extend both your right arm (with the palm parallel to the ceiling) and your right leg (with the ankle flexed) toward the ceiling. Then slowly bend and lower the right arm and leg, bringing them close to your body, and at the same time, extend the left arm and leg.

Do the complete movement (including both sides of the body) three continuous times. Then slowly lower your left arm and leg, and slowly release the tension in both arms and legs. Bring your feet back to the floor one at a time, straighten your legs, and bring your arms to your sides.

Rest on your back for five to ten minutes, breathing gently and evenly through both nose and mouth, and expanding the sensations awakened by this movement.

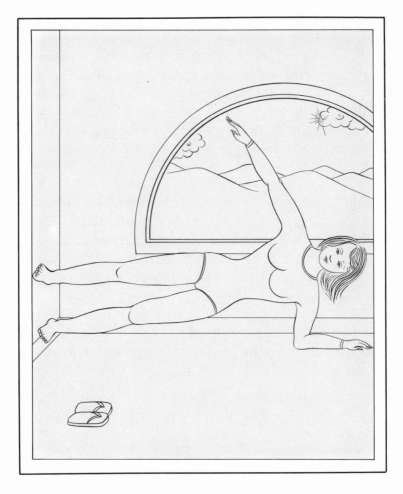

Exercise 108   Touching the Present Body

Find a smooth wall with plenty of space in front of it.
Lie down on your left side with your left arm overhead on the floor, the palm down. Rest your head on
your arm, and with the legs straight, place both feet
flat against the wall, about six inches apart, with the
left foot next to the floor. Support yourself with your
right palm on the floor near your chest, raise your

head and upper torso, and bend your left arm at the elbow, bringing your elbow closer to your body until the bend in the elbow makes a right angle, and your forearm rests on the floor, with the palm down. Then rest your right arm along the right side of your body.

In this position, breathing gently through both nose and mouth, push your *left* foot against the wall, and lift your left leg and hip off the floor. The right leg stays relatively relaxed. Hold a few seconds, then slowly bring your hip and leg back to the floor and rest briefly, expanding the feelings stimulated in your body. Notice the quality of your breathing. Then roll slowly onto your right side, and repeat the movement, this time pushing the right foot against the wall.

Do the complete exercise, first one side and then the other, three times, resting briefly after each side. At the end, lie on your back and rest for five to ten minutes, continuing to expand the sensations awakened by this movement.

A variation of this exercise is to lift the upper arm toward the ceiling as you lift the hip and leg.

This exercise relieves qualities of inner holding and inner chill, and creates lightness in the body.

Exercise 109   Wholeness of Energy

Lie on your stomach with your legs a comfortable
distance apart and your face turned to one side, with
the cheek resting on the floor. Stand on your toes and
place your palms flat on the floor near your chest,
with the elbows up. Keeping your chest on the floor,
lift your pelvis as high as you can without straining;
walking your toes toward your pelvis will help to lift

it higher. Be sure not to put too much pressure on your neck. Hold the pelvis up for fifteen to thirty seconds, breathing evenly and gently through nose and mouth.

Then slowly lower your pelvis to the ground, relax your feet, turn your head to the other side, and place your arms at your sides. Rest briefly, expanding the sensations stimulated by this movement. Do the exercise three times, resting on your stomach after each repetition. At the end, roll over onto your back, bend your knees, bring them close to your chest, and clasp your arms around your knees. Rest in this position for five to ten minutes, continuing to amplify and extend the sensations in your body.

A slightly more difficult version of this exercise is done with the top of the forehead on the floor.

Exercise 110   Energizing Body and Mind

Lie down on your back with your arms extended to your sides at shoulder level, the palms up. Bend your knees slightly, bring your feet together with the footsoles on the floor, and open your knees as wide as possible. Be sure that most of the sole of the foot stays on the floor, although the inside of the foot will lift slightly. Now lift your pelvis as high as you can, so your weight rests on your shoulders and feet. Breathing softly through nose and mouth, hold this position for one to three minutes. Your legs and pelvis may quake a little. Be aware of any changes in your breathing.

After one to three minutes, slowly lower your pelvis to the floor, straighten your legs one at a time, and bring your arms to your sides. Rest for a few minutes, expanding the feelings stimulated by this exercise. You may feel heat between the shoulder blades, and sensations of opening or clarity in the lower energy centers. Do the exercise three times, resting after each repetition. At the end, draw your knees toward your chest, put your hands on your knees, and rest in this position for five to ten minutes.

☆ A variation of this exercise is to lift the chest instead of the pelvis. Lie on your back with your arms relaxed at your sides, your knees slightly bent, and your feet together. Open your knees wide, keeping your feet as flat on the floor as possible. While lifting your chest with the help of your elbows, bend your head back so you can rest the top of your head on the floor. Then stretch your arms out to your sides at shoulder level, with the palms up.

Hold this position for one to three minutes, breathing easily through both nose and mouth. Then very slowly bring your arms to your sides and support your weight on your forearms, straighten your neck, lower your back to the floor, and straighten your legs one at a time. Rest for several minutes, expanding the sensations stimulated by this exercise. You may feel sensations of opening in the chest. Do the exercise three times, resting after each repetition, and for five to ten minutes at the end.

Exercise 111   Circulating Energy

The position for this exercise is somewhat delicate
and requires a subtle kind of balance; you will find it
easier to do some days than others. Lie down on the
floor on your stomach, with your legs slightly apart,
your arms at your sides, and your head turned to one
side. Lift your feet a little and stand on your toes. In
this position, gently raise your knees, thighs, and

lower abdomen (up to about four inches below the navel) an inch or more above the floor. Your upper torso remains in contact with the floor. There will be some tension in your hips, and in the area of the sacrum, but your chest, shoulders, and throat should be relaxed, and your breathing easy and effortless; through both nose and mouth. As much as possible, relax also the backs of your legs.

Tighten your belly slightly and hold your breath back a little, directly in front of the sacrum; this will help to generate energy. Concentrate lightly on the base of your spine. As soon as you feel a sensation there—perhaps warmth or a delicious kind of healing energy—slightly increase the tension in your sacral area. Keep your knees straight. Do not tighten too much—if you do, breathing in the chest will become difficult, you will have to breathe quickly and heavily, and the energy will become clouded and diminish. You need to find a place of balance, not strained and not too loose; then certain feelings are generated within the body. Your chest and throat should be relaxed, the area beneath the navel (both front and back) a little tense, and your breath light.

The sensations follow a slow inner path from the base of your spine up through your belly and chest to your throat and head. Within the head, this healing energy curves back to the spine, passes into the nerves of the spinal cord, moves down the length of the spine and spinal cord to the sacrum, enters the lower energy centers, and then again begins the circle up within the body, turning like a wheel.

Once you feel the energy flowing in this circular path and are able to maintain it, hold the position for three to five minutes. Then gently sink to the floor and rest for three to five minutes, continuing to breathe in the same rhythm as before. Turn your head to the other side if you wish. Then again elevate your legs and lower stomach and continue the turning of the energy wheel for five to fifteen minutes.

If you are not able to contact this energy, separate your knees slightly—this automatically creates a little more tension in your first and second energy centers, generating more energy which then moves to the back of the sacrum where you can feel it. At the moment the energy goes to the base of the spine, be very careful not to tighten your chest. Your chest should be loose and almost still. If you do not experience this energy physically, then imagine it; you can discover a very joyful and refreshing feeling.

If you have difficulty lifting your lower body from the floor, do not strain, but just breathe very subtly, holding your breath a tiny bit in your stomach and at the back of your spine near the sacrum. Imagine your lower body lifting as if drawn up by a magnet. If you breathe too heavily, you will not be able to feel the energy flow in your spine. Loosen your stomach—very heavy tension there can also make this position difficult to do.

Should you have difficulty holding your legs and lower energy centers off the floor for the whole five to fifteen minutes, then lift them up for a shorter time, even a few seconds. Let your lower back be as loose as it can be in this position. If you find it difficult to lift your knees, then stretch your legs as if to lengthen them, and the knees will come off the floor. If you still cannot hold the position, let your knees touch the floor, but make sure that the lower energy centers do not press the ground heavily.

If you are unable to hold this position at all, then just lie on your stomach and be very relaxed. Gently feel the energy rising from behind the base of the spinal cord, moving forward to the lower part of the stomach and up into your chest. Feel the flow of energy relaxing your chest and throat. Follow the energy up inside your head and back under the skull to the spinal cord. Warm energy rises there and passes slowly down the whole length of your spine.

Resting afterwards is an integral part of the exercise. Sink slowly to the ground and rest on your stomach for at least as long as you have held this position, experiencing the movement of feeling and energy within you. After resting, roll onto your side, bend your knees, draw them up toward your chest, and very slowly come up to a sitting position, supporting yourself with one hand on the floor. This exercise may affect your sense of time, and it is important to move very slowly, and with awareness, as you sit and stand. Before standing, move your head slowly up and down, and from side to side, to relieve any tenseness there.

This exercise releases energy blockages (including sexual blockages) in the lower energy centers, and distributes this energy throughout the body.

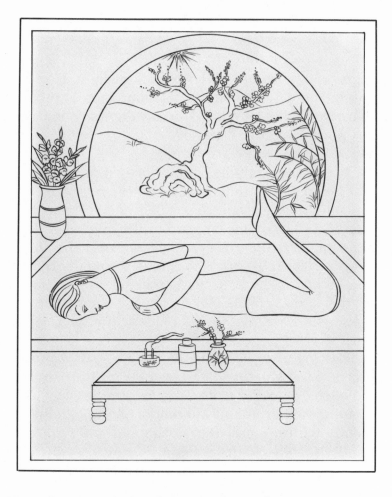

Exercise 112   Stimulating Balanced Energy

Lie on your stomach with your face turned to the left
and your cheek resting on the floor. Separate your
legs a comfortable distance, bend your knees, point
your toes to the ceiling and bring your heels close to
your buttocks. Place the top of your forehead on the
floor, and put your palms on either side of your chest,
so your fingers meet in the center of the chest.

Keeping your forehead on the floor, use your hands and arms to slowly lift your chest as high as possible off the floor without straining. Hold this position for thirty seconds to one minute, breathing evenly and gently through both nose and mouth.

Now sink back to the floor, slowly releasing the tension. Turn your head to the right side, straighten your legs, bring your arms to your sides, and rest briefly, amplifying the sensations stimulated by this movement. You may feel warmth in your chest and tingling sensations in your lower back.

Do the movement three times, resting on your stomach after each repetition. At the end, roll onto your back, bend your knees and bring them to your chest, clasp your arms around your knees, and rest for five to ten minutes, continuing to expand the feelings in your body. If you wish, straighten your legs and rest your arms at your sides.

Exercise 113   Tasting Bliss

Lie on your stomach with your head turned to one side, your legs a comfortable distance apart, and your arms at your sides. Bend your knees and point your toes toward the ceiling. Place the top of your forehead on the floor, and put your left palm on the left side of your chest, and your right palm on the right side of your chest, so the fingers meet in the center of the chest.

Now move your feet in the direction of your head, and your head in the direction of your feet, so the spine arches backward. Do not strain—move only so far as you can without forcing. Hold a few seconds, then gently return your body to the floor. Turn your head to the other side, straighten your legs and relax your feet; bring your arms to your sides, and rest for a few minutes.

Do the movement three times, using the resting period after each repetition to allow the feelings stimulated by the exercise to expand throughout your body. At the end, roll onto your back, bend your knees and bring them to your chest, clasp your arms around your knees and rest for five to ten minutes, continuing to expand the sensations within and around your body. If you wish, straighten your legs, and rest your arms at your sides after a while.

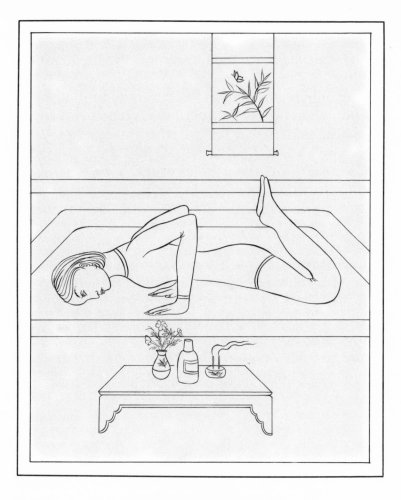

Exercise 114 Utilizing Expansive Energy

Do this exercise on a carpeted floor, and put a small
pillow under your head. Lie on your stomach, and
rest the top of your forehead on the pillow. Place your
palms on the floor near the sides of your chest, with
your elbows up, and your fingers pointing forward.
Separate your legs the width of your pelvis, bend
your knees, and point your toes to the ceiling. In this

position, push your hands against the floor and lift your torso off the ground as high as you can, so your weight rests on your knees, forehead, and hands. Be sure your forehead stays on the floor. Hold for a few seconds, breathing through both nose and mouth as evenly and gently as you can. If you begin to shake, bring the breath and the shaking together and release tensions. Then slowly lower your body to the floor, turn your head to one side, straighten your legs, relax your feet, bring your arms to your sides and rest for a few minutes, expanding the sensations generated by this movement.

Do the exercise three times, resting on your stomach for a few minutes after each repetition, and for five to ten minutes at the end. This exercise may take you to a certain place of intense energy. Feel especially the sensations in your abdomen, perhaps feelings of warmth and a sense of expansion, and distribute them throughout your body.

Exercise 115   Wholeness of Body and Mind

Do this exercise barefoot on a carpeted floor and use a small pillow for your head. Lie on your stomach with your arms extended to your sides at shoulder level, with the palms down. Separate your legs a comfortable distance, and rest the top of your forehead on the pillow. Lift your feet a little and stand on your toes. Bend your elbows, and slide your hands along the floor toward you until your forearms are vertical. Your fingers will point out to the sides.

Now brace your toes against the floor, press your palms and forehead against the floor, and hoist your torso and legs off the floor. Then quickly walk your feet toward your head and roll your head a little, so the top of your head rests on the pillow. Hold for thirty seconds to two minutes, breathing evenly through nose and mouth. Then lower your body to the floor, walking your feet back until you can rest first one leg and then the other on the floor. Turn your head to one side, bring your arms to your sides, and rest for a few minutes, expanding the sensations generated by this movement.

Do the exercise three times, resting briefly after each repetition. At the end, rest a minute on your stomach, and then roll onto your back and rest for five to ten minutes, continuing to extend the feelings within and around your body.

Retreat

Everything you do
can be a beautiful ceremony,
a dance of appreciation.

Once or even several times a year, a brief retreat in a natural setting can greatly expand your practice of Kum Nye. Four days every season or one week a year in the mountains, or perhaps near the ocean or a river, are helpful.

During the retreat, be outside as much as you can. In the morning, practice breathing for about an hour. Sit in the sitting posture, gently open your mouth and nostrils, and breathe very, very slowly, holding your belly in a little. Open all your senses as an invitation to the living energies around you to enter your body. Let your whole body, even your toes and hair, sensitively feel the energies of the cosmos—the light, air, earth, plants, water, and sky; be as sensitive as a fish in water.

Feel the energies flow into you, and visualize the positive healing qualities of all living energies collected in your body. Mix your feelings with these energies, and then let the feelings and energies stream outward from you to the cosmos in an ongoing exercise, a continuing interaction, a circular dance of energy.

Continue this process of healing enjoyment while sunbathing twice a day for about twenty-five minutes (not more than forty minutes at a time). After sunbathing or before sleeping, do an hour of massage, rubbing the oil into your body when you finish. Massaging outside with sesame oil can be an especially delicious experience. During the day, whenever you wish, practice one or two movement exercises you want to develop, and remember OM AH HUM from time to time.

During the time of the retreat, and throughout the year as well, sleep for seven or eight hours a night, and eat simple, balanced meals. Do not place too great an emphasis on food, but whatever your diet (and this will depend to some degree on your childhood diet), lighten it a little, and let it be about sixty-five percent vegetarian. Vegetables, nuts, and fruits are healthful, as are soybeans; it is best not to eat white flour or sugar. (If you want to pursue the subject of diet, the many books available on nutrition can give you more information.) Chew slowly and thoroughly, enjoying fully the tastes and textures of your food, and leave your stomach half-empty when you finish a meal.

During all of your activities, try to be always relaxed, mindful, and concentrated, bringing body, mind, and senses together. In this way, everything you do can be a beautiful ceremony, and all aspects of your life can be transformed.

Index

During five summers, health professionals from many parts of this country attended the Human Development Training Program at the Nyingma Institute where they learned about Kum Nye. Yet my deepest wish has been that the benefits of Kum Nye could be made available to everyone, a wish which these volumes have now fulfilled. May Kum Nye bring increasing joy and fulfillment to your life.

Tarthang Tulku